Your Ministry's Next Chapter

THE PASTOR'S SOUL SERIES
DAVID L. GOETZ • GENERAL EDITOR

The Power of Loving Your Church
David Hansen

Pastoral Grit
Craig Brian Larson

Preaching With Spiritual Passion
Ed Rowell

Listening to the Voice of God
Roger Barrier

Leading With Integrity
Fred Smith, Sr.

Character Forged From Conflict
Gary D. Preston

Deepening Your Conversation With God
Ben Patterson

Your Ministry's Next Chapter
Gary Fenton

LIBRARY OF LEADERSHIP DEVELOPMENT
MARSHALL SHELLEY • GENERAL EDITOR

Leading Your Church Through Conflict and Reconciliation
Renewing Your Church Through Vision and Planning
Building Your Church Through Counsel and Care
Growing Your Church Through Training and Motivation

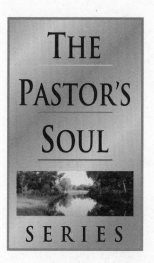

THE
PASTOR'S
SOUL

SERIES

Your Ministry's Next Chapter

GARY · FENTON

David L. Goetz · General Editor

BETHANY HOUSE PUBLISHERS
MINNEAPOLIS, MINNESOTA 55438

Your Ministry's Next Chapter
Copyright © 1999
Gary Fenton

Cover by Dan Thornberg

Published by Bethany House Publishers
A Ministry of Bethany Fellowship International
11400 Hampshire Avenue South
Minneapolis, Minnesota 55438
www.bethanyhouse.com

Printed in the United States of America by
Bethany Press International, Minneapolis, Minnesota 55438

Library of Congress Cataloging-in-Publication Data

Fenton, Gary.
    Your ministry's next chapter : the best is yet to come / by Gary Fenton ; David L. Goetz, general editor.
    p.   cm. — (The pastor's soul series ; 8)
    ISBN 1–55661–975–8
    1. Clergy—Office.   2. Middle aged persons—Religious life.
I. Goetz, David L. II. Title. III. Series.
BV660.2 .F46   1999   99–6556
253'.2—dc21

                                                                             CIP

Dedicated to Alta Faye Fenton,
who is an authentic believer,
a faithful and fun wife,
and a fantastic mother to our daughters.

GARY FENTON is pastor of Dawson Memorial Baptist Church in Birmingham, Alabama. He is co-author of *Mastering Church Finances* and has served churches in Oklahoma and Texas.

CONTENTS

INTRODUCTION

OCCASIONALLY WE HEAR ABOUT MINISTERS whose careers crash and burn at mid-life. Often the tragedies are the result of foolish or immoral choices—pastors who at fifty act as though they were still sixteen. There are, however, other mid-life tragedies, perhaps no less destructive but likely more widespread, that never get reported: ministers who have slowed down, retired on the job, or stopped growing. They deliver previously delivered sermons. They live off the glow of the spiritual passion of their youth. They have stopped dreaming dreams. They dream only when they push the replay button on their memory file. Their careers, families, and churches gradually become diseased. Since the only symptom is a low-grade temperature, no one calls for help.

Is there another option in mid-life besides a public crash or a private slowdown?

Recently I attended a retirement banquet for a man who served as a pastor and as an educator. When the litany of his professional accomplishments were read, the speaker noted that most of them occurred after he turned fifty. In fact, during a "toast" portion of the program, someone mentioned that it appeared as though he had coasted until mid-life.

"During my first twenty-five professional years," the honoree said in response to his toast, "I was just gaining momentum."

He later used a car-racing analogy to describe his life: "Retirement is not the checkered flag indicating the race is over; instead it is the time when I can lighten my load to travel faster. I am not retiring in order to cease working, but so that I can focus attention on my real passions of teaching, writing, and preaching."

His analogy helped me to evaluate my ministry and to write *Your Ministry's Next Chapter*. In automobile racing, the experienced driver often reaches his or her highest speeds during the final laps. Ideally, the driver tries not to carry surplus fuel in the fuel tank. Unused fuel only slows the car down in the most critical stage of the race. In the last few laps there may be a few dents on the body of the automobile and the tires may have less tread, but too much is at stake to coast.

I want the second half of my life and ministry to use all the fuel God has given me, so that with age, I can increase my effectiveness and serve God with passion until my last breath.

Soon I will celebrate the thirtieth anniversary of my ordination. The setting in which I now serve is much different from the small rural church in which I was ordained. On the Sunday afternoon of my ordination, they had to close the windows of the sanctuary to keep the smell of the neighbor's hog pen from distracting the participants. Today, I would have to drive twenty miles from my present church in a suburban setting to find a farm animal. Attendance at my ordination service was less than twenty-five, the average attendance in my current church's adult Sunday school classes. I doubt more than two attendees in that ordaining congregation had a college degree; several church leaders didn't even have high school diplomas. I now serve a well-educated congregation, with doctors, lawyers, and all sorts of business professionals.

Yet my ministry settings of yesterday and today have much in common: Both churches read from the same Book, sing "Amazing Grace," dedicate babies, celebrate weddings, grieve at funerals, baptize in the name of the Father, the Son, and the Holy Spirit, and use the Bread and the Cup as means of sacred remembrance. The congregations, though different in size and sophistication, still need relevant preaching, spiritual instruction, compassionate pastoral care, and organizational guidance. And even though I am older, I still have the need to be prayed for, loved, and gently corrected.

But am I really the same person I was when I was twenty-three?

I am now better educated, more experienced, and further aware of the vast demands of the work to which I am called. But do I have the same enthusiasm and love for the Lord and his ministry as I did at twenty-three? Or have the years that added polish to my ministry also rubbed off its growing edges? Although I have learned to keep my emotions in check in public, does my soul still weep when a saint dies, a youth rebels, or a soul strays? Have I touched the holy so many times that I am no longer in awe when I stand behind the pulpit, bless the Bread and Cup, and baptize the new believer?

I *hope* I am the same person!

The process of writing *Your Ministry's Next Chapter* has confirmed to me that the stages of life require me to change my approach to ministry but not *why* I do ministry. I was an overwhelmed twenty-three-year-old boy when those experienced believers placed their time-worn hands on my head, but I had no doubt I was starting a sacred journey. There was far more passion in my soul than either knowledge or wisdom in my mind. Even though I was in awe of the ordination moment, I was not frightened. Authentic passion comes not from the excitement of youth or the wisdom of age but from a resolve to be found faithful to the One who is the God of all seasons of ministry. That's how I felt then, and that's how I feel today. I hope *Your Ministry's Next Chapter* is more than an inventory to determine what you need to do differently—to keep from crashing and burning or dying a slow ministerial death. I hope it is a tool that helps you say at mid-life, with confidence and enthusiasm, "It is well with my soul."

Before you continue reading, ask yourself the following questions, which will help you apply my experiences and insights to your specific situation:

1. Is there any evidence that I am disengaging spiritually or emotionally from ministry? How?
2. Have I seriously thought about leaving the ministry in the last three years? If so, what issues triggered the thoughts?
3. In one sentence, how would I describe the next chapter of my ministry?
4. Who in my ministry setting would be delighted to know I am reading a book about my next chapter? Why?
5. Do I truly believe my most effective years are in front of me?

1

STRONG TO THE FINISH

A FRIEND IN HIS THIRTIES told me he was looking for a new church.

"The senior pastor has retired," he said.

"Why change churches now?" I asked. My friend had been on occasion less than complimentary of his pastor. I was also surprised his pastor was retiring; he appeared to be at least a decade away from the threescore and five that usually mark retirement.

My friend replied, "My pastor is retiring, but not resigning. He has stopped leading and stopped studying, but he continues to do enough pastoral care to survive. My family and I are in one of the more stressful stages of our lives, and it doesn't appear the level of our anxiety will diminish any time soon. We need a pastor and a vibrant church, not a curator at the museum of the faithful."

After our conversation, I thought about my position. I realized my friend's pastor was three years older than me, and I was forty-nine at the time. I expected close to twenty more years of effective ministry. Would people ever say that of me? Or worse yet, were they already saying that of me? Although our church was growing, I did know of a young family that had left our church to join another—one that had a younger pastor. Their stated reason was that the church was closer to their home, but was that the real reason?

I wallowed in insecurity for several days, but then convinced myself my concerns were unfounded. That incident, however, made me realize that what was said of my friend's pastor could potentially be said of me. So I began to examine my ministry to look for signs of decline. I was determined to place my soul under a microscope and see if the nearly half century of living and the twenty-five years of serving as a pastor had taken its toll. Was my ministry negatively affecting the people I was serving? When I entered ministry I had to analyze issues such as ambition, giftedness, family, and study habits. Now I needed to reexamine my call under the lens of experience.

I determined to visit with effective ministers well into the second half of their ministry. I wanted to know how others were keeping their sword sharp, their soul strong, and their spirit vibrant. My study would not be academic; my concern was not simply to garner information but to learn how to keep my ministry effective.

Reclaiming motivation

In the early years, my call was almost always interpreted in the context of career. It governed my choice of college, my major, and my lifestyle. Although I never liked to use the term *career* when preparing for ministry, my experience—and that of my colleagues—was not that much different from that of teachers, lawyers, and business professionals. The "called" attend college, and perhaps seminary, and seek to prepare themselves to do ministry—and make a living for their families like everyone else. I can admit now that making a living was a much greater factor in my preparation for ministry than I would have cared to admit while in my twenties.

Did I major in religion at a denominational school only from a desire to be better equipped? Or was I aware that it would be the first step in the ministerial career track? Was that extra graduate degree solely motivated by a desire to take the quality of my ministry to a new level? Or was it to take myself to a new level of reward and recognition?

Revisiting our preparation for ministry can be painful: some of our original motives might not have been as pure as we thought at the outset. Yet it doesn't necessarily mean we took a wrong turn. For pastors, there is a relationship between career and call.

When we think about our childhood, we tend to imagine ourselves as cute kids or striking teenagers—until we look at the pictures of ourselves. We easily forget how awkward we were, how big our ears were, that our front teeth made us look like Bugs Bunny, or that we were not spared complexion problems. Yet those pictures don't invalidate our childhood or our youth. In the same way, revisiting our original call can be discomforting but also confirming.

I can remember the struggle in my soul to pursue

journalism and then politics. But God was directing me elsewhere. I remember how I felt—it was agony—when I realized that I had to tell someone that I knew God wanted me in the ministry. As a young man, I exaggerated the grief of giving up my dreams of journalism and politics (I had no real understanding of either career). In my mind, I was forfeiting a Pulitzer Prize or a seat in the Senate. Even years later in ministry, on a blue Monday morning when Sunday's nickel and nose count had been down, I would console myself with what I could have been. Today I can say, though, that my call to ministry was not an emotional response to a series of unusual circumstances. Nor was it out of fear God would strike me dead if I didn't become a preacher. My call came with a deep sense of *oughtness* that I acknowledged to be God's invitation to ministry. Now as I look back, I can say that all I gave up to follow my call into pastoral work were some late nights writing advertising copy and delivering concession speeches after local school board elections.

Yes, I had given up some career aspirations to serve God in the local church, but revisiting my call helped me to remember that my initial "yes" was not as dramatic as it had seemed. Nor was I as naïve as I had feared. Amid the angst and complicated motivations of a young man in his twenties was the definite call of God.

In addition to serving as pastor of a church, I am an adjunct instructor at a seminary. I often hear students speak about their call to ministry. They tell how some window of opportunity unexplainably closed as the window of ministry opened. Or they speak of emotional experiences—the breakup of a relationship, for example—that pushed them in a new direction. Yet when I hear effective pastors in their fifties talk of their call, there is less emphasis on the emotion and the circumstances surrounding the decision to pursue ministry, and more emphasis on their sense of oughtness and purpose. It was freeing to realize, as I reflected on my initial call, that mine was not primarily to make a living as a minister but rather to do ministry. I am fortunate because I can provide for my family as a minister, yet I know if I had to seek other employment, it would not end my ministry. I would find a place to serve without pay, because my call to minister is more my identity than it is my profession.

Remembering and revisiting the call and the preparation from the perspective of maturity can be affirming. Here are several questions that have helped me in that process:

1. *When did I first become aware of God's call in my life?*

2. *What was happening in my life at that time that affected my understanding of God's call?*

3. *How has my understanding of my call affected the way I conduct ministry?*

There were likely factors of which we were not aware then, but that we understand now. One minister told me it was not until recently that he could admit that his parents' divorce made him more aware of God's call on his life. He assumed in 1970 that if he went into the ministry he could divorce-proof his marriage, that somehow by serving in the church he was abandoning his life to God and that God would reward him with a strong marriage. His awareness now of this hidden agenda did not negate his call then, but it helped him unpack some baggage he had carried with him into both his ministry and his marriage.

Redefining the call

Recently a fifty-eight-year-old minister told me, "I am not doing what I thought I was called to do, but I am what God called me to be—a pastor. I thought preaching and studying would be my primary duties, but I find I am leading and relating more. I do prepare and preach weekly, but those activities don't define my ministry. For the last several years, I have felt guilty that preaching was not my passion, but now I see my call was not to a task but to the process of shepherding the church."

Ministers are always redefining their call. Since the church is a dynamic body, the specific needs of the church are always changing. Ministers go through seasons in which they are primarily care-givers, seasons when they are perceived to be proclaimers of the Word, and times in which they serve primarily as administrators. Although these diverse roles bring variety to a minister's activities, they can also create some cacophony in the soul.

Ministers frequently ask themselves, *Is this what I was called to do?*

Several years ago, two retired ministers were honored at a banquet for the contribution they had made through the years. They were asked what advice they would give to men and women who were at an earlier phase of their ministry. The gentleman who spoke first addressed the need to guard study time. He warned how committee meetings, hospital visitation, and counseling appointments could steal time from the task of sermon preparation. He said to avoid interruptions at all costs.

The other gentleman, in his late eighties, agreed sermon preparation was a high priority, but warned against the dangers of preparation: "If you spend all that time in the study and you end up preaching the same claptrap you did before you went into the study, the church may tell you to go to committee meetings and visit the sick because you preach better there than you do behind the pulpit. Remember, there are many ways a minister proclaims scriptural truths."

Yet the question "Is this what I was called to do?" cannot be answered without first dealing with "What did God call me to be?" During the early years of ministry, when the exuberance of youth tends to make us think God wants us to "save the world for Christ," we may be so task-driven we don't see God's call in terms of "being"—that is, developing our souls.

This past year I returned to a church where I had served earlier in my ministry. The congregation was celebrating its 150-year anniversary, and it was affirming to hear what my family and I had meant to them. But I was amazed at how little they remembered of what I considered to be my major role in ministry. One woman told me how significant my visit was to her after her father died. Another person remembered a hallway conversation I had with him regarding his son. An older gentleman spoke of a talk we had at an evening football game, when he told me about the death of his son ten years earlier. Only one person told me his life had been changed by a sermon, which was titled "Why Jesus Would Not Join This Church." Although I was familiar with the sermon, I had not preached it. A guest speaker had delivered the message at a church banquet!

The idealistic energy of youth is often framed in the context of tasks. Our youth drives us to answer questions, solve problems, and fix what we think is broken; maturity helps us to determine the right question, discern if there really is a problem, and know if something is broken. An older minister recently told me he spent the first fifteen years of his ministry answering the question "Did God create the heavens and the earth?" only to realize the people were really asking, "Why did God create me?" But this minister did not look back regretfully on the early stages of his ministry. Instead, he used his newfound discovery to rethink ministry strategy.

Ministry in my forties was a time of deliberate and sometimes painful redefinition. Early on I had worked to develop my speaking and writing skills. Yet I was often disappointed at the results, which could be summarized as "more was said than done." I motivated people, but I didn't lead them anywhere. When I realized this, I understood better some of my earlier frustrations.

The churches generally supported the direction and vision I cast, but I saw few tangible results. I assumed our failure to achieve was either because of their lack of commitment or my ineffective communication.

Now I realize I wasn't much of a leader; I was weak in helping the churches I served *implement* their vision. That insight is redefining how I think and go about pastoral work. Recently, God placed me in a situation in which I needed to be more of a leader: I had to move from the role of cheerleader to quarterback. As a result, my preaching and pastoral care changed. My study time and method of exegetical work didn't change; I continue to work carefully with the text, but my application has changed. Before, I put a lot of emphasis on inspiring people on Sunday mornings; now I see inspiration as only the first step in leading people to service. I involve staff in the process as well as laypeople.

I redefined my call.

Redefining our call is not so much spiritual surgery in which we take a scalpel and scrape away some hidden malignancy; rather, it is a time to bless our past, learn from our mistakes, and look toward the future.

A small town football coach spoke recently at a civic club I attend. He has coached in the same school system for nearly twenty-four years, with little hope of being invited to move into administration or to coach in a larger system. He was asked how he kept his love for his job, even though he was now coaching the sons of players he had coached in the earlier years of his career.

"When I start to forget why I'm coaching," he said,

"I simply spend more time with the players after the games. I need to see the disappointment on their faces after the losses and hear the laughter after they win.

"But if I hang around with spectators, I tend to wonder why I'm in this."

After many years in church work, it is possible to spend too much time with the wrong people—local church bureaucrats, for example, who sit in leadership positions, content merely to observe the ministry of the church. The best way for me to reenergize my call is to spend time with non-Christians who are searching for God in all the wrong places, new Christians enthusiastically throwing themselves into the life of the church, or hurting Christians who desperately want to find their way back into the fellowship of Christ and his people.

The call to ministry *can*, after mid-life, be certain. The call *can* propel you as it once did. *Your Ministry's Next Chapter: The Best Is Yet to Come* is about the rediscovery of the call to serve God with passion and focus. The rest of this book is devoted to rediscovering that call in the various spheres of pastoral work.

2

STAYING ON THE JOB

I KNOW OF A MID-LIFE MINISTER who loves to fish. He not only enjoys fishing, he is a good fisherman, according to those who can evaluate the sport. He spends a significant amount of time reading about fishing and searching the Internet. He says he has finally learned, in middle age, to enjoy life, but several of his church leaders have said that he has finally learned how to *avoid* life. This pastor devotes so much time to his hobby that his ministry appears to be suffering. He, like others at mid-life, seems to have succumbed to the temptation of distraction—all in the name of "getting a life," or finding a hobby outside of the church.

After twenty-plus years in the local church, a pastor who finds the pace getting faster and the body growing more weary may wrestle with some tough questions: What do I do with the next half of my working life? Have the blessings outweighed the burdens? Do I still feel that inner fire that once drove me? If not, how do I recapture it?

It's tempting to try to escape the issues of mid-life rather than work through them. This temptation, of course, is by no means unique to the ministry; it is one of the crucial issues we face as we grow older. Although I have not done a scientific study, I am not sure career restlessness is any greater in the ministry than in other care-giving professions—or any profession, for that matter. All of us grow weary of the daily grind. There is a certain loss of energy and enthusiasm that comes at mid-life. Some pastors fight this loss by working harder, only to find that doing so does not relieve the pain; it only increases the misery, the desperation, and the loneliness.

Others leave the ministry completely, the most obvious way to escape, and find another way to make a living. When I have visited with ministers in their mid-forties to early fifties, I have found many had seriously considered other lines of work. A friend who has served three churches for a total of thirty years told me that not a week goes by that he does not look at the Want Ads section of a major city newspaper.

I asked him why, and he replied, "Some days I think I can't continue to endure the criticism and the pressure."

Yet seeking another way to make a living is not necessarily an attempt to escape life. For many who serve as pastors in the local church, ministry is their life, not their livelihood. Some at mid-life, for a variety of reasons, simply move to another means of making a living, but they are not forsaking their calling. A pastor in our area recently resigned his church and opened his own business. Yet he preaches every Sunday at a small church and is helping it to discover a fresh vision for its community. Because of his spouse's health and the fact that he has two children at the university, his financial needs required him to find another line of work. Was he escaping ministry? I don't think so. Ministry is a way of life.

From what I have observed, most pastors who leave the church in mid-life do so for two reasons: (1) They have a strong sense of call away from church ministry. As they have walked faithfully on the journey of ministry, God calls them to new opportunities. It is not an abdication of duty to go in a new direction. This is not walking away, but being led away. (2) There are personal, family, emotional, or physical health problems, necessitating a change in what he or she is doing.

An acquaintance recently left his church and started a new career. His wife's emotional and physical well-being were directly affected by ministry in the local church. Although he could have made some adjustments in his style of ministry, he said he left the ministry in order to keep his marriage vows. To stay would have hurt his wife. Was that an escape? Yes, but in the sense that the Old Testament Exodus was an escape. We don't criticize Moses for leaving Egypt. Ministers need to be cautious in condemning those who enter other professions at mid-life. In some cases those who are leaving may be taking the higher road.

Escape routes

Then again, leaving the ministry *may* be an attempt to escape life. We're tired of the hassles, the weekly grind, the lower pay than our contemporaries with similar levels of education.

When we were young, most of us may not have even known that escaping from life was an option. But by the time we reach the end of the second quarter of life, we not only know it is an option, we know several ways to escape without appearing that we are abdicating our calling and profession. Some pastors, in effect, quit even though they are still working.

My fisherman acquaintance, whom I mentioned in the opening paragraph of this chapter, tells his friends in the church he has finally found a hobby and now he can minister more effectively. Some in the church say he fishes away, rather than deals with, the stresses of the ministry. From the amount of time spent with his hobby, it appears he is trying to escape the discontent of ministry. He is likely on a collision course with the church leadership. He is going into the battle carrying the flag of well-rounded life, while his opponents say he has hoisted the white flag of surrender to the pressures of life. According to the church insiders, his well-rounded life will probably roll to a new location soon.

Another person in ministry, a staff pastor, announced to his church he no longer would neglect his wife and children, that he would be taking more time off to spend with them. Yet when his wife went to see a counselor about her marriage, she said his hours away from the office were not spent with his family but with his computer and the television set. According to him, the pressure of his work was so great he needed the diversion of the keyboard and the remote control.

Other ways of escape may be much more subtle but just as damaging to ministry. One, of course, is workaholism—the "acceptable" form of escape to many church attenders. Some pastors defend their unholy work habits with holy language: "God is blessing my ministry." Many pastors neglect important areas of their lives, especially in the early, career-building stage of ministry.

A twisted outcome of workaholism can be martyrdom. A pastor who is now retired was overworked and underpaid during his years in ministry. He rarely took time away from work for his family or for himself. By his poor example, he inadvertently created a great amount of pain for his young successor, who is seeking to be more balanced. The retired minister never confronted the church about its apparent lack of concern for his family, and is now angry that no one intervened on his behalf. He accepted the suffering as his lot in life. He still attends the church and visits parishioners, who comment warmly on his ministry, but who also say, "Poor Brother 'Do-good.' He has done so much in his life, and he has had it so hard." He is, in effect, attracting salve for his wounds. His behavior helped foster a martyr culture in the church. The church has taken on his personality, and although the economy of the region is good, the church sees itself as a poor, struggling church. The church has more than a year's budget in reserve, but still pays its pastor less and expects more than in comparable churches in the county.

There's a fine line between being a martyr and being a victim, between suffering for the cause of Christ and casting oneself as somehow holier because of the heavy duties that go with ministry. The pastor with a victim mentality can find this style of living and ministry falsely rewarding. Seeing ourselves as victims, though, is a self-centered way of living.

I'll mention one more temptation, a form of quitting or retiring on the job, which I will discuss further in a later chapter: Mid-life can also bring the temptation to *specialize*. This can be another form of escape. The upside of maturity—working out of our strengths and wasting less time trying to buttress our weaknesses—has a downside.

"My gift is preaching," someone might say. "I don't have time to do pastoral care anymore." Or, "My gift is pastoral care. I'm going to preach somebody else's sermons. My church will understand, because I am a caring pastor."

Most of us who serve local churches cannot, with a few notable exceptions, become pure specialists. I serve a relatively large church, with a staff that covers many areas, and yet I preach, do pastoral care, handle some counseling, and give some administrative leadership. Granted, I don't do nearly as much in each area as I did when I served a smaller church, but I still function regularly in areas outside my expertise.

This has been a surprise to me: I thought that as I matured I would be able to serve primarily out of my strengths, but I have come to the conclusion that to serve a local congregation is to be a generalist. I am not suggesting we ignore our natural giftedness or our spiritual gifts, but in most churches a legalistic interpretation of spiritual giftedness does not work. And those who try to focus solely on their giftedness in the second half of life may be trying to escape the full role of pastor.

Such escapism can lead, of course, to more destructive behaviors, such as an addiction to pornography, drugs, or alcohol. I have heard of ministers who justified these sins because they felt they were so holy most of the time that they had a right to a private life!

The answer, of course, is not to escape life but to embrace it.

Getting a life

Instead of checking out at mid-life—either by leaving the profession of ministry or by retiring on the job—we must distinguish better between our calling and our profession. We are called to serve God. Our profession is only a part of that—a significant part, but not the whole. This distinction can help us redefine joy. When we were younger, joy often came wrapped in an adrenaline rush, and was often work-related. Can anything compare with the "high" we experience during the half-hour of preaching, when we realize we are communicating the Word of the Lord effectively? Or what can compare with the sense of joy that comes from helping someone make a good decision, or comforting someone in a time of sorrow or hurt? Yet what happens when the gate to the pulpit is locked because we have been terminated? Or when our ministry of care is not performed as an official member of the clergy?

One key to sorting through our calling and profession more clearly lies in accepting our life as a gift from the God who wants us to experience life abundantly, wherever we are. Relaxing on a beach with my wife, Alta Faye, can bring a sort of divine joy, just as preaching to an Easter crowd can. It is a different kind of joy, but a holy joy nonetheless.

Several years ago Alta Faye and I had a swimming pool put in our backyard. I worried about what people would think if the pastor had a pool, so I explained to the key church leaders what I was doing—even though we owned the home and didn't need their approval. One of them said, "If you want my approval you're not getting it."

Disappointed, I said, "Maybe I shouldn't do it."

"I didn't say that," he replied. "If you're waiting for my approval, you're not getting it because you don't need my approval. You work hard. It's your money. Whether I think it's a good investment of your money has nothing to do with it."

The pool was built, and it turned out to be a wonderful gift for our family. We moved two and a half years later, but as an investment in our family, the rewards were incalculable. It was, in essence, the first step toward our family's "having a life."

Another key to help rethink the relationship between our call and our job is to learn to enjoy certain experiences for their own sake, rather than as a vehicle for ministry.

I've always enjoyed Friday night high school football games, but in years past I would only go to support the players and their families. Sometimes I went to make contacts with prospective members or absentee members. Especially when I was serving a small church in a small community, almost every act could be leveraged into "ministry." I would seek to turn an ordinary event into something holy to advance the kingdom. But as I reflected on my motives, I realized my Friday night ministry was more often related to my ministerial career than to doing any good for the kingdom. I wanted people to know what a great and caring pastor I was.

One night I was in the stands at an exciting football game. Ordinarily this would have been a lot of fun for me, but I saw three people on the opposite side of the stadium with whom I wanted to make contact. I became so consumed with how I could "conveniently" bump into them after the game that I missed out on the game itself. On the drive home, I thought, *This isn't right. One, it's hypocritical; and two, I'm miserable.*

On another Friday night, the weather was bad and I didn't relish sitting outside watching a game, but I told my wife I still planned to go.

"Why?" she asked.

"I need to," I said.

"Why do you need to?"

I was honest with her: I had a work-related agenda in mind—on a night I had declared to the church to be personal time, a night when I did "what I liked." I had turned my going to a football game into something I *needed* to do. I have found that ministry can take place if I don't force it. But if I determine I can do ministry and have fun at the same time, it is usually neither. I began not to take every Friday night so seriously.

A friend—not a pastor—tells a story of being in San Francisco in 1989 during the earthquake. He was at a conference with a group of ministers, and the hotel, although it wasn't damaged, was shaken. The next morning at breakfast he asked one of the ministers, "What was your first thought when the building shook during the earthquake?"

One answered, "I was trying to think how I could use the experience as an illustration on Sunday morning." And he wasn't chuckling.

When my friend told me the story, he said, "How ridiculous." I laughed and feigned agreement, but inwardly I was thinking, *What's wrong with that? I probably would have had the same thought!* While I'll always be a preacher looking for a good illustration, I don't want that to define me. I've begun to see that my profession as an ordained minister is not the same as my calling to serve God. He will use me as he chooses.

Healing wounds

Another component that can help us not to check out of ministry in mid-life is to monitor more closely the pain that comes as a result of local church work.

Over time the bruising and battering endemic to and pandemic in the local church can build. If that happens, we will want only to escape.

I have recently come to know a retired minister, an articulate gentleman who seems at peace with his ministry and at ease with the world. Most of his ministry was in a different part of the country in affluent churches. I assumed he probably had enjoyed a comfortable ministry. But he recently told me of the church that terminated him after less than nine months. It was a large church, and its leadership maneuvered a long-time staff member to replace him. He told me some of the warped rationale they used to justify his termination. When I remarked to him that he did not seem to be bitter about it, he said, "I determined my call and my gifts would be my identity and not the position I held. I was old enough to know what to do when I was wounded."

It is true that by mid-life we should know how to recover when we are wounded. There is a difference between withdrawing and going deeper into our spiritual reserves. The fact that we have been wounded does not indicate a lack of spiritual depth, but taking on an attitude of martyrdom and victimization does.

I find at age fifty I have to work more diligently at not feeling sorry for myself than I did at thirty-three. When a young minister is wounded, there is always some dear saint ready to anoint his soul with the balm of comfort. But at fifty, pastors don't receive so much slack from churchfolk. It's as if they are saying, "At his age, he should have known better." A question I now ask folks who hold me accountable is, "Am I giving any evidence that I'm feeling sorry for myself?"

Much to my dismay, on occasion they say yes.

Balance over time

I want to mention one more aspect of rethinking our work in the second half of life: balance. At mid-life, more than at any time since his ordination, it may be possible for a pastor to lead a more balanced life. His family is grown, and the learning curve of ministry skills is not so steep.

However, balance may not be the most practical goal to shoot for. There will be seasons when our lives won't be balanced, and we need to be able to live with that, at least temporarily. Accomplishment takes effort, focus, and a selective neglect of other priorities. A concern for balance alone can lead to a kind of mediocrity. Thinking about a balanced life must take place in a larger context—it cannot always be neatly packaged into weekly or monthly segments.

A pastor in a stressful church situation once told how he kept himself emotionally healthy. During a controversial building campaign, for instance, he focused on the task at hand and postponed other pastoral duties, even some family issues. When it was over, he changed his pastoral style and also spent more time with his family. I was younger when I first met him, and I asked him how he kept his composure and energy.

"If you looked at my ministry through a micro-scope," he said, "you would think it was unbalanced, but if you looked at my ministry through a telescope you would have a different picture. There are times during the year when folks think I'm lazy, and other times when I'm accused of being a workaholic." In a sense he was advocating a short-term plan of imbalance but a long-term plan of balance.

In 1996 our church went through a major fundraising campaign for our building program. It was the most intense five-month period of my ministry. Not only was raising money difficult, some neighbors of the church began a high-profile attack on the zoning for our building. I neglected some pastoral duties and postponed some family tasks to handle the crisis. I knew the capital funds campaign would not last forever, but if it was not done right, I, and the church, would be feeling the effects for a long time. The campaign ended on June 6, and our family took off for the beach on June 7. For the following three weeks after vacation, I deliberately kept a lighter schedule; my life balanced out over time. In the fall of that year I picked up the pace of pastoral care. The key to balance is to look at the big picture.

I'm slowly learning that I'm a person before I'm a pastor. The older I get, the more I realize how sweet God's gift of life is. Not long ago a friend from church died of a sudden heart attack. He was forty-seven. His children and mine are the same age. It was a sobering moment: *If I have a heart attack, my death will be no more or less significant to God's kingdom than his was.* At one time

I would have looked at his death and thought only of the tragedy, but as I thought about his life, I saw grace and joy. Yes, he died too young, and his children still needed him. But he also lived and experienced joy.

With God's grace, I hope I can do the same.

3

NEW FUEL SOURCE

ERNIE BANKS, THE CHICAGO CUBS Hall of Famer, is known not only for what he did on the baseball field but also for what he never had the opportunity to do. Banks never played in post-season games or in the World Series. The other National League teams discarded the Cubs like chewing gum wrappers; the Cubs were permanent residents of the cellar. Yet every season Banks excelled as both a hitter and a fielder and never gave evidence of less effort.

Recently in a radio interview, Banks was asked how he could play at maximum level when there was little or no hope of playing in the World Series. He responded with a classic line: "You have to love the game itself and not love yourself in the game."

Banks went on to explain that he loved the game of baseball so much that he had to give his best effort every time. Yet he said some only love the game in the moment of play, and not for the love of the game itself. If a player plays with the attitude that his season will be over in August, he will simply go through the motions, even though he has to play another month or more of games.

That can happen to pastors too.

In the early years of serving churches, many of us live in anticipation of being discovered. While avoiding any show of ambition, we believe it won't be long until the wise and perceptive denominational executive will realize that even though we are young, we ought to be serving in the "Jerusalem" of our denomination. Or the search committee from the metroplex will unexpectedly hear us and discover homiletic paradise by our pulpit light. When we hear the words "too young or not enough experience," we believe that a few more Decembers will take care of that; that is, a few more gray hairs and we'll be ready for the big time. When we feel unappreciated, the confidence that we will be discovered keeps us going. We sincerely desire to honor God, but believe we have something to offer the work of the kingdom that few others have.

Then without warning the current shifts.

The "youth" that once cursed us is now the blessing for which the religious crowd clamors. After we get turned down for a new position, word filters back to us that the denominational executive and the search committee said they were looking for someone younger. How could that be? Just yesterday we were too young. Then the hard question gets raised: What fuels us down the road to excellence when we realize we will never be "discovered"?

In the corporate world, older and more mature executives are often replaced by younger, more energetic managers who will work for less money. Many in our churches know the pain of being too old to advance and too young to retire. There is little evidence that the ecclesiastical thirst for youth is related to financial concerns. Few churches try to cut payroll costs by seeking younger, lesser paid ministers. Their desire for younger ministers is more likely related to the search for energy and image.

Some pastors may address the image issue with tanning beds, hairpieces, and plastic surgery, and end up in the second half of their ministry looking like aging Las Vegas entertainers. I prefer not to go in for a ministerial makeover. I believe mid-life can be a good time to examine and overhaul our ambitions and let God redeem our work for his glory.

Smoldering fire

The issue of ambition has always been thorny for ministers. Our Lord addressed the issue frequently. Even though he faced it head on with his disciples, at least two of them continually struggled with a desire for recognition.

We can deny ambition exists and allow it to subtly destroy the right purposes for ministry, or we can even justify our attitude and allow ourselves to believe that God really does want to bless our egos. But both of these approaches are forms of denial and allow the smoldering fires of ambition to go unattended. As a result, the smoke produced by unbridled ambition can cloud our vision for ministry. We need to admit and channel our ambitions rather than allow them to direct our work.

I can't address fully the complexity of pastoral ambition in only a chapter, but I want to focus on the drive to do well in church work that is fueled by the desire to hear "Well done" from people we esteem highly. Early in my ministry, the comments of parishioners as they went out the door was my measuring rod for the quality of my preaching. Once I was given a note after a service that had been handed to an usher. It read: "Outstanding message today. Good content and fantastic delivery. I am sorry I didn't get to tell you in person." The note was signed by a person who was running for public office. After watching my "Aw shucks" response, the usher told me the person handed him the note after the music portion of the service—he had not stayed for the sermon but had gone on to hear the minister at the larger church one block away!

Not all comments have secondary motives, but the ultimate goal for pastors should be to move from being motivated to do well because of what it will do for us to being motivated to do well so God will be honored and the work of the kingdom advanced.

An older minister told me he recently reviewed his sermon notes from when he was in his thirties. He said he was surprised both by how good some of the sermons were and how bad others were. He said he realized that earlier in his ministry he was more dependent on emotional inspiration for his sermon preparation than on prayer, disciplined Bible study, and wisdom.

By the time we hit forty, most of us know how to

generate praise and acceptance by our preaching. For example, I know certain kinds of illustrations evoke in people a "warm-fuzzy" moment. But they may not need a mood-elevating illustration at the time I would like to give it; rather, they may need to hear an accurate exposition of Scripture. As I reflect on the sermons given in my youth, I must admit I often surrendered excellence in exchange for acceptance without knowing I had done so. That's a hard thing to admit.

Discovered!

There are, of course, no "three easy things" that will reset our motivations in the second half of life to serve in the church with passion and integrity. A lot of spiritual development comes through reflection and personal insight—often during and after pain. Overcoming ambition happens when I stop thinking about who I *could be* and realize who I *have been* for all these years.

Twenty years ago the act of ordination did not mean as much to me as it does now. Then I saw it as one more hoop to jump through in order to get my preacher's union card. I didn't seek to discredit the process of ordination, but it seemed somewhat perfunctory to me to have a group of aging ministers tell me what God and I already knew: I was called to preach. How many people have to discover us before we feel validated as ministers? Reliving the act of ordination has helped confirm to me who I am.

During my early forties I received a call from a friend

who told me that a large church had lost its pastor and that members of its search committee had called him about me. They indicated to him their interest in me and that they would be contacting me soon. Although I was not sure I wanted to be pastor of that church, I definitely knew I wanted to be asked. It was a church that had all the ministries I wanted to lead. To know the church of my dreams was interested in me, or at least considered that I may be in its league, salved my ego during a season in which a small group from my church was questioning my leadership abilities.

Several days later a secretary in our office received a call from some friends in that church telling her the rumor was rampant—I was going to be the next pastor. I was flattered but I knew that rumors and reality are two different things. In the following weeks I heard several times that I was a front-runner for the position. Even the chairman of deacons of the church I was serving asked me not to leave. I told him that I had not as yet been contacted and that if I were I would make it a matter of serious prayer. I also learned that the search committee had several well-known laymen in the Christian community serving as members and that the chairman was a high-profile man whom I would be honored to meet. Whether or not I became their pastor, my meeting with their committee was going to be a highlighted page in my mental scrapbook.

Several weeks later, I received a call from a denominational executive who congratulated me on my move "to this great church in America." I asked him what he knew about the situation, and he said that the media and the church had been alerted that the search committee would make an announcement in one week. He had inside information that I was going to be the man. I informed him that unfortunately his information had no basis in fact. No member of the search committee had ever contacted me and they had never requested my résumé. If I did become their pastor, it would become known as the "immaculate selection" as there had been no contact.

"Are you telling me these folks never considered you as a serious candidate for their church?" he said.

Later a friend sent me the information the search committee had given to their church. This committee of Christian heavyweights had interviewed more than twenty qualified candidates in the process of finding the one God had prepared for this position. It didn't hurt my ego to know I was not asked to be their pastor, but it was tough to swallow, given all the hype, that I wasn't even in the top twenty.

After I learned of the decision, I returned to my study to finish the message for the midweek worship service. Humbled, I told myself I would rather be in the will of God than in my dream church. I grieved that I never had the opportunity to meet the committee. Then I looked at my ordination certificate hanging on the wall and saw the names of the ordination council— Tom, Roy, H.A., and Gerald—layleaders, deacons, and bivocational ministers who had served in a rural county. I remembered their affirmation by laying their hands on me and blessing me and I realized I had been discovered.

When a congregational body or denomination licenses or ordains a person into the ministry, it is acknowledgment that a discovery has been made. Ordination validates us as viable ministers of the gospel. It is in the context of the corporate body and the laying-on of hands that the church confirms and publicly affirms the God-given abilities and call on our lives.

Full speed on every play

Once we give up the expectation of yet being discovered, we are free to serve God with passion and renewed energy. A college football coach recently explained how his team had progressed in its approach to games. He said that in his first year at the school, his team had tried to keep the game close until the fourth quarter and then hope for a major break like a fumble or a pass interception to turn the momentum of the game in their favor. Now, the coach said, the team plays at full speed every play because they are not waiting for the breaks—they know their best is required every moment to win the game.

Authentic ministry does not depend on our getting a big break; instead it rests in the awareness of God's call to ministry and the daily offering up of our best efforts as an offering of gratitude. No longer do we have to live our lives waiting for our big break. Ministry is not a competitive sport, it is a cooperative effort. Knowing that you have done your best brings a wonderful sense of reward to the soul.

Last year I helped a man in our church who runs a small business. He was understaffed for a major event he was sponsoring. I took a few days of vacation to help him and worked in his warehouse, did over-the-counter sales, answered the phone, met with sales representatives, and put in several fifteen-hour days. I did things I did not think I could do. The experience exposed me to a side of business I had never seen before. When the event was over, I was exhausted and exhilarated. In the days to come I analyzed why I had such positive feelings about such difficult work. Although there were several contributing factors, one key reason was that I knew I had done my best in an area for which I was not equipped.

To some extent, the sense of significance that arises out of ministry should flow out of our inadequacy. While I've been in pastoral work for many years, I am still an amateur. Every day I am in over my head—whether meeting with a young father considering divorce, a highly respected businesswoman who is thinking about bankruptcy, or an eleven-year-old boy who is interested in making his public profession of faith. I simply do my best. That may seem a little simplistic, but when I start to compare myself to others, my efforts lead only to exhaustion.

I have since recognized that seeking to preach and minister in an excellent way for an audience of one—my Father in heaven—is much more liberating than operating out of a response to what others say about me. I would have tipped my hat to that truth as a younger pastor, but only now that I am older can I admit to my misguided motivations. Although I can still find myself at times seeking the praise of others, affirmation is what I really need—affirmation of who I am and what I have been called to do. When someone calls late at night and says, "I need someone to pray for me and with me before I tell my mother that my father died at the hospital"— that is a great affirmation of who I am and what I am doing.

4

NOW THAT I'M A GROWN-UP

WHEN I WAS A YOUNG PASTOR, I would regularly go up stairs two at a time. I was gifted with energy, enthusiasm, and optimism—the hallmarks of youth. I made calls three nights a week, preached Sunday mornings, Sunday evenings, and Wednesday evenings, and I believed there was no problem our church couldn't solve.

I was pastoring in Tyler, Texas, when an incident made me realize that I could not go on like this forever. Every Wednesday I spoke at a noonday luncheon for businesspeople, an event that drew about two hundred. One Wednesday my adrenaline was not pumping; I was dragging throughout the day. Later a staff member said, "You're not doing real well, are you."

"I'm doing fine," I said. "Why do you say that?"

"I watched you go up the stairs at the luncheon today. You were really laboring. There was no energy in your step—but when you came out in front of the group, you really turned it on. You can't keep doing that."

I tried to dismiss his concerns by saying I was having a tough week. But as I thought about it later, I realized that recently I had taken the back way on Wednesdays so no one would see me trudging in. I was tired, and it was not just from hard work. I knew I had to conserve energy for my presentation. I was not a twenty-five-year-old anymore.

Hard-wired pastor

To the young, God gives physical energy and optimism. In mid-life and beyond, he gives wisdom—which helps us know best where to put our energies. But because the church tends to reward the upbeat, go-getting attitudes of youth, a mid-life pastor faces a crisis when he realizes he can no longer "run up the steps," when his energy begins to flag as never before. He may view this change as loss. When this happens, there are usually three temptations: fake it and try to hide any sign of weakness; decide to slow down and coast; quit.

The optimism of youth is a wonderful thing, but it doesn't always make for the most effective pastoral care. When I was twenty-seven I visited great numbers of people who hurt in some way. In my unbridled optimism and lack of life experience, I may have minimized the pain of life. Maturity, however, has brought depth and perspective, which enhances pastoral care.

Recently I visited a woman in the final stages of cancer who was forced to live in hospice care. As I left her and her family, I thought about how much differently I minister at fifty-one than I did at thirty-one. I listened to her more than I would have when I was younger; I was more hopeful in the context of the Christian faith;

and I did not feel a need to rescue the family from their sorrow. Whether claiming physical healing for a sick person or being confident that a parishioner would be able to solve an emotional problem, I used to believe in the quick-fix, positive-thinking solution. I was certain that righteousness would win the day, or at least win by the end of the day. When righteousness did not win, my optimism left me. When the person with the problem did not get better, I felt frustrated and disappointed. My emotions rose and fell according to the degree of "success" I saw in my ministry.

I am less optimistic now, but I have more hope, and as a result I believe I am spiritually and emotionally healthier. I believe righteousness wins out—maybe not today or this week or even this year, but over the long term and into eternity. I do not get angry with people when they do not turn their lives around as quickly as I think they should.

Years ago I dealt with a particularly difficult pastoral situation. A man I will call Stephen was trying to overcome a gambling addiction. I invested considerable time talking and praying with him. I referred him to a professional counselor and then followed up with that counselor. Stephen would stop gambling for about three or four months and then fall back into the same negative patterns. I gave up on him many, many times. I often felt angry and deceived by him—a product of the cycle of optimism and pessimism. It took fifteen years, but Stephen, with the help of Gamblers Anonymous, is now living a victorious life. Hope is more long-term and less likely to wane in dark times. That is, I now feel less optimistic about short-term results and more hopeful about healing over time.

The gifts of youth that God bestows on everyone diminish with age. What happens when the energy and enthusiasm of youth begin to retreat? In the last chapter, I discussed the issue of ambition and how recognizing that we've already been discovered by God can help us retread our tires for the second half of our ministry. Yet another part of the retread is accepting the new realities of mid-life and coming to terms with how God has wired us.

Character at the crossroads

At mid-life we stand at a crossroads of character. We have been around the block a few times. Not much surprises us anymore. But no matter how much wisdom and perspective we may have gained over the years, it is easy for us veteran pastors to succumb to cynicism. We have heard so many speakers and read so many books and dealt with so much church politics that we may develop the attitude, *Teach me something new. I dare you.* A church consultant told me about a presentation he made at a gathering of ministers. As he spoke, he noticed that the body language of the pastors over forty-five seemed to communicate, *I already know this.* They had ostensibly grown jaded.

I am acutely aware of the dangers of cynicism because I grew up cynical and a little arrogant. I believed

I was smarter than the system. I could find a shortcut around everything. As a preacher, I also knew that a cynical comment in a sermon could be a great attention-getter, an effective teaching tool—until I was confronted about it. I had used an illustration about a pyramid marketing company in which I basically questioned anyone who worked for them. It was funny, and people laughed. Afterward, an older layman approached me and said, "Gary, you're very good at working cynical statements into your messages that make us think, but eventually it's going to destroy you. Cynicism can make a preacher come across as an angry old man." I took his advice to heart.

Older pastors especially have to be careful how they employ humor and anger in preaching. A twenty-four-year-old can come down hard on sin, alcohol, and promiscuity, and the congregation thinks it is wonderful that this young person has turned away from sin. If a fifty-four-year-old preaches the same way, he may come across as an embittered old man, punishing everyone for the sins he did not get to commit. There is nothing winsome about an angry old man. Humor is an effective communication tool at any age, but the kind of humor we use should change with age. A preacher in his twenties can tell a story about mothers-in-law, and everyone laughs. When the older pastor tells the same story, people think, *Here's a guy who's had a bad experience with his mother-in-law*. Although cynicism may be more natural for the middle years, it fits like a cheap suit on a middle-aged preacher.

GARY FENTON

While writing a Thanksgiving meditation recently for our church newsletter, I thought about the subject of cynicism. I concluded that in essence it is a form of self-centeredness. The cynic thinks he or she is superior in knowledge or is able to judge the motives of others. No wonder cynicism does not wear well on the mid-life pastor. I realized that for me cynicism was a spiritual battle and began to ask God to remove my cynical spirit.

When Zig Ziglar, the popular motivational speaker, came to our church, we invited forty boys from a children's home to hear him. Close to sixty at the time, he connected with the abused nine-, ten-, and eleven-year-old boys. These kids had every natural right to be cynical and suspicious, but they quickly bonded with this optimistic man. Later he and I did a TV commercial together, and I observed firsthand his genuine gratitude in everything he did. As I compared his attitude with my own, I began to see that gratitude can never coexist with cynicism. Rather than praying, "Lord, help me not to be cynical," I asked God to make me more grateful. I have seen that the more deliberately grateful I am, the less cynical I will be.

A spirit of gratitude is one of the key ways to restore passion for ministry—a new motivation for the second half of life. One of the most beloved men in our church is our minister to senior adults. At eighty-six, he has retired three times from the ministry. He once said, "I have never met a happy person who was not also a grateful person."

Journey toward acceptance

Virtually every pastor struggles with feelings of envy or inadequacy. We compare ourselves to the pastor across town whose church is growing faster than ours. We wish we were more skilled in evangelism or in leading a staff. The negative side of me looks at rapidly growing churches and thinks, *That guy is just shallow and superficial.* But the confident side of me, the holy side, thinks, *No, he has the gift and I don't, and that's okay.*

Maturity calls us to the place where we can accept both our gifts and our lack of them and be content. We need to claim our giftedness without despising our weaknesses. In the idealistic, early years of ministry, we tend to believe we will conquer our weaknesses—that is the optimism of youth. We can achieve anything with just a little more effort. But as we get older we come to terms with our blind spot. It will always be there, but God in his sovereignty will use us anyway.

Maturity can help us measure our ministry differently. Success in ministry, of course, is not only about numbers. It is not just about people making immediate changes in lifestyle. It is about faithfulness to Scripture, about the congregation becoming more godly, and about our becoming more godly. The vision statement of the church I currently serve says our church is "to be found faithful as God's people." I have taken that for my own life's mission: will God find me faithful as a Christian, as a father and a husband, as a minister—with all my strengths and all my weaknesses, in my calling now and in the years to come?

Perhaps the question of mid-life is not "What will I be when I grow up?" but now that I am grown up, "What kind of person am I?" Although this question should be asked at any age, we may not have had enough life experiences to ask it until mid-life. The call of youth is tomorrow. But the burning question of mid-life is today. These are the most productive years of our lives. That's why it is critical to know who we are.

It takes time to know where our true strengths lie, and we can go for years—making a lot of mistakes along the way—before we gain insight into our abilities. For a long time I thought I was gifted in counseling because those who came to me with a need would affirm how God had used our time together. But by now I know that counseling is not my gift. Empathy is. I am good at giving people a sense of acceptance and affirmation. I am not so good at going beyond that to help people work through their problems. And I do not always understand how relationships work.

Once I met with a couple who had intense marriage problems. Both liked me and indicated I understood their struggles, but the more I worked with them the worse the situation became. I was not helping them learn to communicate with each other, although each was bonding with me individually. The marriage continued to deteriorate, and my role contributed to the problems. Each quoted me to the other, using my words as a weapon. When the spillover from their hurting relationship began to flow into our church, I realized I needed to step away from the position of counselor to them.

Shortly after that incident, I was in the home of another couple whom I was counseling. Each wanted me to choose sides. Both were manipulative, and I had not perceived their deceptions until it was too late. I also saw how their children were being sucked into the conflict, and I felt great sympathy for them. In a moment of youthful anger, I told the couple I would do everything in my power to make sure neither of them gained custody of their children, even if the kids had to be turned over to the welfare department. I walked out and slammed the door. On the way home, I first felt angry, then, of course, embarrassed. There were no grounds for such drastic steps, and reality hit me: *I have had two failed counseling situations in a row. What does that say about my abilities as a counselor?*

My first instinct was to back away and not get involved with people. But then I began to realize I had confused the gift of empathy with the gift of counseling. Hurting with someone is not the same as helping someone. I began to understand my limitations, and this has freed me to minister more effectively. Today I can say, "I'm not that great at counseling." When I began my ministry at twenty-three, my limited experience in this area would not have warranted such honesty.

Through the years I have confused several characteristics of youth with spiritual gifts: for example, I mistook the excitement and enthusiasm of youth for visionary leadership, because inspiration is a more visible trait of leadership. It is the vision-setting speech that rallies the troops or motivates people to do the work of the kingdom. But true visionaries are also able to carry out the behind-the-scenes work it takes to turn the vision into reality: making phone calls, preparing for meetings, and recruiting the right people for key tasks. I have had to accept my limitations in this area. I am not a natural visionary. I can preach and inspire and help others dream dreams, but I have to force myself to roll up my sleeves and get involved in the nuts-and-bolts of turning vision into reality.

I realized this when our church held a "vision service" in which we presented the goals of the church for the entire year. There was electricity in the air, and I felt as if I were preaching from the mountaintop, tablets in hand. (We all have sermons we will always remember preaching, and this was one of them.) The next day a woman called me, a very perceptive person and one of my strong supporters. She said, "I got home yesterday and was so excited—but I don't know what I'm supposed to do next. It was a wonderful day but there was no strategy. Where do we go from here?"

Frankly, I did not know where to go next. I had thought that was someone else's responsibility. The risk of being a visionary without a strategy is that discouragement can set in when nothing happens. I was stunned at the realization of my weakness in leadership in this area.

The 90/10 principle

While I have gained more insight into how I am wired, at mid-life, I have had to face another reality. I prefer to work out of my giftedness, to concentrate my efforts only in areas of ability and interest. But ministry often falls under the 90/10 principle: 90 percent of what I do is what I must do in order to get to do the 10 percent I love to do. For example, I love to preach. The thirty minutes I communicate God's Word on Sunday are most often pure ecstasy. But wrangling with a board or putting out a church fire, which can consume inordinate amounts of time, drains me. I have often wished I could preach 90 percent of the time.

Not long ago I was supposed to meet with a key committee to discuss an important project. I knew what needed to happen, but to do it meant I needed to meet with the committee chair, make some phone calls, and show up at the meeting—basic administrative stuff. I had some other things to do that night and did not relish sitting through another meeting, so I skipped it. I phoned in my input to the chairman. It was a costly mistake. Days later I found out the committee had not done anything, and I wound up having to meet with several key people to follow up. I could have saved myself all that work if I had just gone to the meeting. But that is the sort of thing that consumes 90 percent of my time.

When I was younger, I assumed it was my fault the percentages were so out of balance. I thought if I did things right that somehow the 90 percent would shrink and the 10 percent would expand. Experience has taught me otherwise. Pastors are called to wear many hats. We cannot always operate out of our gifts. God places the pastor where there is a need, and it is his or her job to address that need. But addressing the need eventually makes it possible for the pastor to exercise his or her gifts.

My current church was bitterly divided when I came on as pastor. I knew I needed to build trust and rapport with the congregation, so I spent a great amount of time doing hospital visitation, which does not necessarily allow me to use my gifts. I do not listen as well as I ought and I too often pray with a person and leave quickly. But I knew there was a need I had to meet. Later as the church began to heal from the conflict, I was able to devote more time to preaching.

One key point to remember about our gifts: though they bring blessing, they can also bring great pain. For example, my passion for creating sermons has for years ruined Saturdays for me. The great preacher Gardner Taylor said, "Saturday is agony and ecstasy." On Saturdays I am consumed with looking for that new phrase and creatively tinkering with Sunday's message. I love college football but I can't attend any games because they are usually on Saturdays. I love spending time with my family but we had to shift our family time from Saturday because there was no joy when we did things together. Overall, though, I have a deeper appreciation for God allowing me that 10 percent (which, admittedly, is more like 2 percent most weeks).

"Grace" and "gift" have the same Greek root, and through the years I have become more aware of the connection. No longer do I chafe as much when I cannot operate in my areas of giftedness; now I am more grateful for the time I can spend with it and am amazed that anyone would pay me for what I love to do.

5

ALL-PURPOSE PASTOR

DURING MY SENIOR YEAR IN COLLEGE, I met several times with one of the legends in my denomination. This larger-than-life character pastored a large church, was a noted author, and had an extensive radio ministry. In awe of him, I consciously made him my role model for ministry and studied his work habits. I wanted to be as productive as he was.

On one occasion I asked how he had become effective in so many areas of ministry. He told me that it came with age and experience. His exact words were, "The longer you serve, the broader your ministry becomes. You can't afford to be a specialist when you serve in the emergency room of the soul." I determined then I was going to excel in everything, just as I thought he did.

When I was in my early thirties, I led a conference in the church of an older pastor who became my unintentional mentor. By this time in ministry, I was experiencing some frustration—too much to do and too little time to do it. At the conclusion of the conference, I asked the pastor to critique my presentation. He made some generous comments and then gave me some constructive criticism about my filling the presentation with sarcastic one-liners.

Then he gave me some unsolicited advice.

He told me that if I continued at the pace I was working I would soon burn out. He advised me to choose whether I wanted to be a pastor or a preacher, and that I should make the decision before I turned forty. He was of the opinion that to be effective in my mature years the choice between pastor or preacher must be made—one would be my "major" and the other my "minor."

"Churches will allow you to be mediocre in both areas when you are young," he said, "but once you are in your mid-life, congregations need you to excel in one and bring in people to help you in the other." He had decided to be a pastor, and his ministry gave evidence that his decision had been well made.

Now I had a dilemma: my two role models espoused what I perceived to be conflicting views. One said you can do all things well, while the other said you have to be a specialist. From the perspective of mid-life I can see now that to some extent both views contain truth. An effective pastor develops skills in all areas of ministry but learns how to use these skills at different stages of life. In some seasons of ministry, we may need the honed skills of a specialist, yet in most churches we have to function in more generalist roles. Much of our early years are spent trying to learn the basics, but only in mid-life do we have the skills and life experiences to know when to be a specialist and when to be a general practitioner.

For most it takes until mid-life to become competent in the three key areas of pastoral work: communication/preaching, pastoral care, and leadership/administration. It took me almost a decade per area to reach a measure of competence. Most ministers typically feel more confident and competent in just one area. But when I visited with pastors serving effectively in their fifties and sixties, I discovered most of them had to develop competence in each area over time. Ironically, just at the point of achieving competence, some ministers are tempted either to narrow their ministry to one area or to leave the ministry because the demands appear to be too great. In the previous chapter, I discussed the importance of not retiring on the job, a common temptation of middle age. This chapter defines the pastoral role for the second half of life.

Three-role specialist

When I was in my twenties, I worked diligently on my communication skills but I don't remember consciously making it my first priority. In my denomination, preaching is considered to be the basic skill in pastoring a church and as a result I felt the most external pressure to excel in that area. The church I served during seminary never asked me any questions about my theology or my care-giving skills before they asked me to serve as pastor, but the congregation did hear me preach four times before they made their decision.

My first church after seminary asked some questions about my leadership abilities, but its search committee made it clear that energy and excitement were expected in the pulpit. I don't remember if they were concerned about the content of my sermons, but while I worked diligently on developing communication skills, I also worked on developing content. I never wanted anyone to leave the church on a Sunday morning saying, "He had nothing to say" or "He didn't say it well." I learned to preach without notes, and this discipline alone added several hours to my sermon preparation each week.

To allow plenty of time for study, I learned how to make hospital visits in record time. By doing most of the talking, I could control the length of the visit and make the transition into the bedside benediction before the patient could report to me all the details regarding his surgery. I also learned that if I visited grieving members while they had other visitors I could make a quicker exit. By calculating the time of my visits, I presented the illusion of care-giving. Because I made so many visits, people could not say I neglected them, but because I never took much time with them, neither could they say I helped them. I cringe as I think of the folks I hurried past in the process of economizing hours for study.

My first full-time church after seminary grew

quickly, but I did not know how to lead the church through a building program. While both my immediate successor and I worked on preaching and motivation, we struggled to help the organization take the needed steps to get from A to B. Therefore, the church did not get the badly needed new building and new location until they called a pastor who was strong in administration skills. He may not have been as polished in his preaching, but he accomplished what neither of his predecessors could do. After the building was completed, he was able to enhance his communication skills.

My point is simply that I neglected early in my ministry to develop certain basic pastoral skills in order to focus solely on preaching. Often the communication side of the ministry receives the most attention in our rookie years. But the same problem can afflict staff pastors. One minister of education nurtured his writing skills while neglecting organizational development. He knew the university community in which he served read his newsletter and other printed reports with a magnifying glass but could tolerate classes or programs that were not properly promoted. As a result, his printed pieces and columns in the newsletter were well received but the small groups under his leadership were dying. He had to learn basic organizational skills to better serve and nurture his small-group coordinators.

In my thirties I moved beyond preaching and learned how to be a pastor and provide pastoral care.

Serving in a community with an average age of forty-eight forced me to deal with seeing church growth occur at a slower pace. I began to learn more about the grieving process. I begrudgingly discovered it cannot be accelerated. For a pastor to be a healing presence requires time and listening. Answers given to a dying patient are not as crisp and concise as the well-spoken lines in a sermon. Care-giving thoughts are often refined and revised mid-sentence, without the help of a thesaurus. Although hesitant to think so at the time, my preaching and communication skills did not grow during this stage of my life; perhaps they even deteriorated somewhat.

In my forties, as I mentioned earlier, I discovered I was not a natural leader. I had confused inspiration with leadership. I could motivate people, but despite the enthusiasm I generated in the churches I served, often little was accomplished. Occasional insights and outbursts of vision are not the same as leadership. I had to learn how to communicate vision on a regular basis, develop strategies, and recruit, train, and develop other leaders. I consciously determined to read books, attend conferences, and hold myself accountable in the area of leadership. By pushing hard each day, I tried not to neglect pastoral responsibilities such as hospital visitation, but I became painfully aware that it was during this stage of ministry that I was criticized for neglecting people.

Now in my fifties, for the first time I feel a measure of confidence in all three areas: communication, pastoral care, and leadership. Though I serve in a large church with competent staff members, I find to some extent I must function in all three roles. Rather than becoming a specialist in one of the areas, I must be a specialist in each.

Destined to be a generalist

Although most of us would like to become specialists in one area and outsource the other two, few of us have that luxury. We have to know how and when to operate in these roles and when to shift into new roles. At mid-life we have the accumulated skill-development from our experience to draw on, yet we may be tempted to specialize as we age.

As energy levels taper off, we may tend to neglect what we do not enjoy. That means for many pastors letting the management/leadership part of the pastoral role slide. I intentionally put the terms *management* and *leadership* together because although there is a clear distinction between the two, they often run in tandem in the church. Some pastors resent the management or administrative side of pastoral work. Managing often seems to be unrelated to our call and less spiritual than preaching or pastoral care. As a young pastor, I thought if I could delegate the managerial tasks to someone else and do only the work of a preacher or pastor, I would be happier and the church would be more effective.

Administration is the most difficult role for me, and

yet is crucial to my current church in its particular stage of development. Within a four-year period we started an entire second Sunday school, completed a capital fund-raising campaign and started another, and added mid-week and contemporary worship services. I am confident that if these administrative demands had been made on me at an earlier stage in my ministry, I may have convinced myself God was calling me to another congregation.

In the last few years, I have begun to see the task of management/leadership as a core value of my calling. They cannot take the place of preaching or pastoral care, but since I believe God called me into ministry, he must have been aware of the full responsibilities of my call. If I am to live out my call in the second half of life, I cannot jettison the parts of it that make me uncomfortable. Rather than resenting the administrative side of my call, thinking it is something the human factor of the church has added, I now see it as a gift from God—to be accepted and developed.

Two events were crucial in this shift. The first was when a younger minister with great potential resigned his church because he was not handling the administrative side of things well. After he left, with no other place of service in view, he came to see me. He was starting to emerge from the grieving stage and moving toward accepting some responsibility for his present situation. He said, looking back, he had rarely prayed about his administrative responsibilities, except in times of crisis. He commented that if he ever had the opportunity to pastor again, he would pray for power and wisdom in administration as well as in preaching. I then realized that I had not prayed often about these tasks—other than prayers for deliverance or forgiveness, that is.

The second event that affected my view of the administrative side of my ministry was a conversation with an older pastor who proudly told me he did not invest much of his time in the management of the church. Ironically, I was aware of two families from his church who had recently joined ours. Both had commented how their pastor did not seem to care for or love the people in his church. Theirs were not horror stories of an abusive pastor, but they gave narratives of benign neglect in management. Evidences of this were the declining quality of the facilities and the late arrival of Sunday school curriculum. This pastor was good at one-on-one pastoral care, but his people interpreted administration or management as corporate pastoral care.

Most churches will tolerate the weaknesses of their pastor and staff, but they tend to resent ministers completely neglecting one or two of the three key roles. The model of the small-town family doctor is the model many churches unintentionally use for their pastor. Prior to managed care and HMOs, the family physician knew enough about all the areas of medicine to discuss most illnesses. The minister who does not have a basic competency level in communication, pastoral care, and leadership may be perceived as at best incompetent and at worst uncaring. In the early days in America there was a great similarity between the country doctor and the country parson. One cared for the body and made house calls. One cared for the soul and did home visits. Both the country doctor and the country parson were seen as wisdom figures in the community; people stood in awe of their commitment and stamina. While in the last thirty years the medical profession has moved from the rural family doctor who did a little of everything to the specialist who concentrates on his or her narrow field, most pastors today must function as generalists. That means we must continue to grow in our giftedness, but shore up the other parts of pastoral work that we tend to slight.

Cutting through the denial

There is potential for crisis if a pastor does not know his or her strengths—something we should be pretty confident of by mid-life. Sometimes a pastor will be in denial about what he or she is good at doing. A leader from another congregation met with me regarding his pastor and wanted to know how he could help him. The congregation, he said, loved its pastor; he was an outstanding care-giver and an adequate leader. But he imagined himself as an outstanding communicator!

This church's leadership strongly disagreed with his self-assessment. Some board members had gently suggested that while he was working on his doctor of ministry degree, he also take some classes in preaching. He resented the suggestion, and some of his key laymen were afraid he was going to resign over it. Apparently he had rarely allowed input on his performance.

I can empathize with the tendency not to want to hear bad news. It is still difficult for me to invite and accept performance evaluation, but I do not want to stop growing in the second half of my life. If the best is truly yet to come, then I must be willing to fight through the pain of self-development.

I do believe, however, that I am more capable of handling performance evaluation now than I was twenty-five years ago. In the early years I did not always know how to properly assess the evaluation of others. If I liked the person who was offering the criticism, I would accept it as valid; if I did not like the individual, I would reject it as petty or irrelevant. But through experience I have discovered that my friends can be wrong and my enemies can be right. I have also learned—albeit begrudgingly at times—that most evaluation or criticism is partially true, and I gain the most if I am willing to endure the pain of sifting through it.

Recently a woman wrote me regarding three grammatical mistakes and one mispronounced word in a Sunday morning sermon. Although they were not major mistakes, they were indeed mistakes. I can remember a time when I would have either ignored the letter or found a kind way to tell her I was sorry she had missed the central point of the message. But I read the letter and concluded she was correct. I called her and thanked her, and she worked with me on the word I had wrongly pronounced for years. The following Sunday I used the word in my sermon for her sake and for my mine. I received an anonymous note in the offering plate that read, "Praise God, after nearly seven years of being our pastor you finally said 'escape' correctly."

Inviting evaluation has never been easy for me. An older minister recently urged me to set up a system for evaluation. Although our deacon board is not directly responsible for pastoral oversight and supervision, its members are more reflective of the age demographics of our church than any other elected body. So every other year I meet with our forty-eight deacons in small groups and ask them three questions: (1) What does the pastor need to know about his performance or the performance of the staff? (2) What are the challenges the church is facing? and (3) What appears to be going extremely well in the life of the church?

For the most part the response is affirming, but occasionally some direct and painful comments are made. On one occasion painful comments came from a frequent critic of mine. Unsure how to evaluate his remarks, I asked one of my friends for his opinion. He helped me see there was some truth to the negative evaluation.

"If you felt the same way as my critic," I said, "why didn't you tell me?"

"I didn't think it was a significant enough matter to burden you with it."

Without inviting the evaluation, I would have never corrected something that was actually easy to change. While everyone tips their hat to personal development, growth is painful, especially in mid-life, when we have years of ministry experience. We must resist the temptation to plateau. To those who continue to push the outer limits of their potential, the best may be yet to come.

6

STAYING IN THE LOOP

A PASTOR I KNOW HAS SERVED the same church for more than twenty years. His staff members joke about the yellowed notes he takes into the pulpit. They call Sunday mornings "golden oldie time at pulpit city." The pastor was an effective preacher in the '70s, but at some point he stopped growing and starting repeating. His sports illustrations are out of the '60s and '70s. During the unbelievable summer of 1998 when Mark McGwire and Sammy Sosa kept America counting as they raced to break the Roger Maris single season home-run record, this pastor used illustrations about Hank Aaron.

Apparently he did not realize that many in his congregation had no idea of Hank Aaron's contribution to baseball—that his lifetime home-run total surpasses even that of the legendary Babe Ruth. This preacher's points are good and timeless, but he wraps them in yesterday's news, so his preaching does not connect well with a large portion of his audience.

At any stage of life, an effective preacher understands the times and discerns the winds in popular culture. Of course, that is much easier to do when we are in our twenties and thirties, because we are a part of the youth culture that defines the buzz in music, literature, the arts, and sports. In the second half of life we naturally tend to move from the center of our culture, and it is easier to lose touch. While the biblical text never changes, our audience does.

The point of staying hooked into popular culture—and thus into the world of our listeners—is not to come across as hip but simply to communicate clearly the gospel. At mid-life we cannot be something we are not—thirty years old. And we must do more than merely re-fine techniques and skills we learned twenty-five years ago. If we are developing only our skills—and not grappling with the new paradigms for communication—we are like an anesthesiologist trying to improve her skill of administering ether. Nobody uses ether anymore—and hasn't for years.

I have discovered two levels we need to monitor: the macro level of the culture and the micro level of our own experience. Throughout *Your Ministry's Next Chapter*, I've warned against the mid-life temptation to decelerate from life and ministry. The following chapters focus on the art and skill of preaching, ensuring through our communication that the gospel is presented in all its fullness.

Facts vs. feelings

In mid-life it is critical for preachers to continue to develop their understanding of culture. Avoiding the "Hank Aaron syndrome" requires that we become alert to the language of the day, the vocabulary and experiences common to contemporary society. For example, the lighthouse is a traditional religious metaphor for something that helps one avoid danger and arrive safely to port. In previous eras that image may have been understood by most congregations, especially those along the coastal areas. That is not the case today. "Keyword" is a contemporary word that comes from the world of on-line. A keyword is a shortcut—type it into the search-engine box, and the user can go directly to a website or on-line area. A keyword acts as a guide to help a person avoid getting lost in time-consuming searches. "Keyword" is a better term to use than "lighthouse"— both illustrate truth but one is fresher.

On television, I recently heard Billy Graham, now in his late seventies, and noticed he used computer terminology several times. He spoke of something being "byte-sized," and he used the word "rebooted." Clearly Graham is doing his homework on what communicates to his audiences, and that is part of the reason he has been so effective for so long.

Subscribing to a variety of magazines has helped me to stay connected to the contemporary culture. The magazine *Wired* deals not only with the business/technological world but also with the younger generation's desire for no boundaries in life. Although its audience is well-educated, this magazine reveals how widespread antigovernment feelings are in our country. The paramilitary mind-set of the rednecks who play soldier in the isolated parts of rural America is really not that much different from the technology geeks who band together to oppose any attempt to censor material on the Internet. The desire to remove limits imposed by authority is the common thread tying these two groups not only to each other but to many people in our congregations. Philosophically this magazine does not fit me at all but it helps me to understand the spirit of the age.

Even the advertisements in *Wired* are teaching instruments. These printed commercials are designed to touch the emotions of the reader. They are image-driven. This is a key cultural switch from years ago when words were primary. My generation appealed to the rationale in order to get to the emotions; the present generation tends to appeal to the emotions to earn the right to address the rationale.

I also try to read a couple of bestsellers every year. I ask church members what they are reading, and if I find several mentioning the same book, I try to read it and identify the issues it addresses. About three years ago I heard people talk about the Dilbert books. I was unaware until then how much frustration people were feeling at work. I not only preached on the subject but invited a guest speaker to address the futility people experience at work. What folks were suffering because of downsizing and rightsizing was more than worry about job security. They felt betrayed and bitter; as though they were pieces on a chessboard.

Although my first choice is not fiction, I also try to read one popular novel each year. Sometimes I have forced myself to write a book review of it, so I can get my mind around the major moral issues involved. I must admit this has been rare. A group of ministers in our community formed a book club and meet once a quarter to hear a review and to interact with its ideas. I also make it a habit to take younger people to lunch and pick their brains for ideas. Asking them to explain what they do for a living is a major education. I discovered that specialization in the work market is far greater than I realized. In the process of staying current, I have also learned how deep the spiritual thirst is in our society. Even white-collar professionals often feel like pieceworkers at a factory. With today's technology, most people work only with one small ingredient of a large complicated recipe. They struggle to see the larger meaning of what they do and how they fit into the big picture. As a result of this knowledge, I preach on finding meaning in life much more than I used to.

Strategic emotion

I grew up in the '50s and '60s in what some call "*The Weekly Reader* generation." *The Weekly Reader* was a little black-and-white newspaper distributed in grade schools that kept students informed on current events. Conventional wisdom of the '50s told us that facts were going to form the future, so the magazine was filled with facts. As a generation, we tended to trust facts and mistrust emotions, and that may have affected our religious views as well. Emotional religion was for the uneducated and unbelieving, and religious teaching focused on the factual proofs for Christianity.

I learned that as a preacher I needed to prove factually that biblical principles "worked." If the Bible commanded us to honor our father and our mother so our days on earth would be long, I validated that injunction with statistics showing that people with happy families lived longer. While feelings could be manipulated, facts were the sixteen-penny nails of our faith.

But things have changed. The generation behind me, often called Generation X, tends to trust feelings over facts. Its young men and women know that facts can be manipulated, that there can be information without knowledge. Madison Avenue knows this well. Think of the Nike commercials on TV: they don't tell you anything about the product or the price. Nor do they compare Nike shoes with any other athletic shoe. They touch your emotions, showing Michael Jordan hanging above the rim while you hear the roar of the crowd. And that communicates to you that Nike makes a great shoe.

The use of image to evoke emotion and thus action has serious implications for the preacher. In a sense, the ability of a preacher to evoke emotion in a Generation Xer—not in a manipulative way, of course—can help gain credibility and drive home the truth of the gospel. I know a pastor who sometimes weeps during his sermons, and it has been fascinating to hear the different reactions of people in his congregation. One woman, embarrassed by her pastor's emotion, said, "My pastor cries during his messages. Do you think maybe he's having an emotional problem?" On the other hand, I've heard younger people say, "Man, he's real. He's got the stuff."

My point here, of course, is not to imply we should use emotion irresponsibly or ignore reason. I am simply trying to buttress my thesis that, on a large scale, the way people think has shifted in recent years, and the mid-life pastor needs to continue to grow to be effective. Nor am I saying we should eliminate facts from our preaching. Rather, we may want to use emotion strategically in our communication to increase our effectiveness—especially with younger listeners.

In 1998 the Birmingham, Alabama, area lost thirty-four people in a tornado during Holy Week. A thousand homes were destroyed and hundreds of people were injured. On Sunday morning the newspaper ran photos of all thirty-four victims on the front page. The paper also included stories about each of the victims. The tragedy was on people's minds as they came to church, and I needed to speak to their hearts about how this event could possibly fit into the message of Easter.

I began with a story about a wedding I performed in the 1980s. At the rehearsal, the whole wedding party was downcast and the bride was crying. I assumed her emotion was because of the normal pre-wedding jitters. As I was leaving the church to attend the rehearsal dinner, the bride and groom asked if they could talk with me. As soon as the bride entered my office and shut the door, she burst into uncontrollable sobs. I asked her what was wrong.

"My father found out this morning that the biopsy report was positive," she said. "He has a malignancy. It's a fast-moving cancer and he doesn't have long to live—and he's walking me down the aisle tomorrow."

Then the groom said, "How do you rejoice when you really want to cry?"

I told that story on Easter Sunday and repeated the question: "How do you rejoice when you want to cry?"

"It's been a long and hard week in Birmingham," I continued. "This morning all of us sat around our breakfast tables and looked at the pictures of thirty-four individuals. We wept as we read the stories of those people between the ages of two and eighty-nine who died this week. There's a side of us that says, 'I really find it difficult to celebrate Easter today.' But we don't have any choice. It's Easter. We're Christians. And we are supposed to rejoice."

I went on to tie our story in Birmingham with the story of the first Easter in Palestine, how it had been a devastating week in Jerusalem—the lives of at least three people had been taken, the lives of the disciples had been shattered, and yet there was a wonderful promise from Jesus. I had to work hard not to make the rest of the sermon a manipulative, emotional monologue. I avoided the temptation to say, "Don't you all want to be ready for Jesus when the next tornado comes?" Instead, I discussed the meaning of the Resurrection.

My point is the placement of the illustration in the sermon—at the beginning. If I had preached that same message in 1975, I might have ended the sermon with a story such as the one from the wedding. But because of the cultural shift from reason to emotion, I placed the moving story at the beginning. I needed first to connect with my audience, and then bring in the facts of the Resurrection.

However, there is still a place for rational apologetics in our preaching—the "Jesus was either a liar, a lunatic, or Lord" approach. The mid-life seeker connects with that. She wants historical evidence for Jesus. The young adult seeker, however, tends to ask different questions. He says, "I want to know there is a spiritual reality. I could live with it being a myth, but I want to know it touches my soul."

I am finding I have to use more "spiritual" terms in my preaching now. Twenty years ago pastors tended to stay away from such language because we were afraid of sounding churchy. Many non-Christians feel comfortable with spiritual language, even though they may not know the reality behind it. Recently a woman asked if she could have lunch with me and one of my associates. She said she had an important question she wanted to discuss: "Can I become a member of the church without becoming a Christian?"

She had been attending church because she loved the spiritual aspect of our ministry—she apparently sensed the presence of God and enjoyed learning about prayer. She also liked our children's programs. But she was struggling with the role of Jesus. At lunch, she told me she had difficulty believing Jesus was the Son of

God, so we talked about the uniqueness of Christ. We continue to talk to this day, as she explores the truth of Christianity. I speak to her out of reason and logic, but what initially drew her into our church was its appeal to her heart and soul.

Even with the advent of emotion over reason, I have discovered that young people are much more confrontational today than they were when I was growing up or even than they were fifteen years ago. Many in my generation, while they might have disagreed, would not likely challenge a pastor's authority publicly or even face-to-face.

But today young people will say openly, "Pastor, I don't agree with you."

My style, which in the past honored diplomacy, has mildly changed. Although I am not an "in your face" preacher, I am more direct than I was a few years ago. At one of our contemporary services recently, I spoke on the issue of homosexuality. I stated strongly that homosexual behavior is wrong. But with equal directness, I said that too many Christian teenagers feel justified in harassing and even beating up homosexuals, and this is as offensive to a holy God as homosexuality is. In fact, I said, both the homosexual and the one harassing him stand guilty before God.

When I finished, some of the older people said to me, "You came down harder on those ridiculing homosexuals than you did on homosexuality itself."

I responded, "How many homosexuals do you think we had here tonight?"

"Hopefully, we didn't have any," they said.

We probably did, but I let it go and said, "How many people here, do you think, have ever ridiculed or harassed a homosexual?"

"Probably several."

"Well," I said, "they were my target audience."

Apparently I hit the mark: a number of the young people I talked with after the service gave me positive feedback, and one nineteen-year-old college student said, "I needed to hear that. I knew it was not right to harass homosexuals, but you said it was a sin."

Who's Barney?

"Don't ever preach that sermon again." Norma Jean's blunt words after the Sunday morning service surprised me, since she was one of my consistent encouragers. The topic of my message had been "A Christian Approach to Death."

"Tell me why," I said.

"It was too hard. Everything you said was accurate, but it cut into my soul because I've just lost my mother. It wasn't that you were insensitive. It was just too harsh."

That was in the 1970s, before I had experienced the loss of someone close to me. I had spoken on the stages of grief in a Christian context. My exegesis was skillful and the application had seemed on target—but there was no heart in it because I had never lived it. It was clinical, not real.

Later, I learned more about dying, and more about myself. My dad passed away in 1983, and several years later, my father-in-law. As I watched my wife and her family deal with their loss, I realized how unusual was my way of grieving. Not only had I been insensitive to Norma Jean, my parishioner, but when my father-in-law passed away, my unsupportive response was hurtful to my wife.

Several years later I preached the same sermon in a different setting, and it seemed better received. The primary difference was not in the location or even the content but in the preacher. My experience with grief had changed me and my preaching.

Wisdom gained through life-experience may be one of the greatest benefits of mid-life. During the early years of ministry, we have three primary sources for every sermon: Scripture, the work of the Spirit of God in our life, and insights we have gleaned from the text. The result is we frequently preach things we don't really know to be true but that we accept as true from other sources. That's only normal. We've had little life-experience. The young preacher risks sounding like an expert when in fact he has no experience from which to make application. He can sound much like a business consultant who draws his information from the latest book.

But at mid-life, I can preach to young parents with greater integrity because I can still remember on some level what it was like during those years. I may not even use a personal illustration, but I will likely not give a glib illustration that glosses over the needs of young parents. I have a greater sensitivity to their needs because I have been there. I have been a parent of young children.

Life experience deepens our understanding of Scripture and thus shapes our communication for the good. I never understood the relationship between King David and his son Absalom until I had children of my own. I can remember preaching what I thought was a powerful sermon on David's failure with his children. It was creatively titled, "Why the Apple Has a Bad Seed." Yet when a close friend dropped off his well-trained son at college and then saw his moral character degenerate, I grieved with him and that changed my understanding of the David and Absalom drama. When I took my oldest daughter to college nearly a thousand miles away from home, hoping she would choose good friends and make good choices, the story hit me even more deeply.

But here's the temptation at mid-life: to preach from our most recent experiences. Unless I discipline myself, I find I speak from the last five years of my life.

My wife and I are now in the empty-nest stage. We know what it is like to send three kids off to college—it is an immediate issue for us. So I have to make an intentional effort to listen to families who are sending their children off to first grade, or who have a new baby. I knew I needed help with this when our staff was planning a major children's event at church.

Someone said, "We need to have Barney here."

Barney? Barney Fife? I thought. *No, it wouldn't be him.*

"Who's Barney?" I asked.

101

"You don't know who Barney is?" someone replied.

Everyone but me seemed to know Barney was a singing purple dinosaur, a playmate of kids everywhere. I had lost touch. To counteract this, I intentionally visit young couples in their homes. I had always imagined that someday I would pastor a large church where I could contact people by phone and letter, and someone else would handle the home visits. But I have found that for preaching purposes, as well as for follow-up on prospective members, I need to see people in their home environments. It also helps me to understand how a young family works today. The kids bring out their toys and video games. I learn what nine-year-olds talk about. I may then use a video game in a sermon as an illustration.

It is more of a challenge to identify with teenagers. Every year I meet with our graduating seniors—mostly to listen to them talk about high school and some of the tough stuff with which they have had to deal. I always learn something new. For example, one student talked about the number of seemingly good kids who use drugs—sharp, middle-class kids who otherwise have their lives together. Another spoke about the rise of the "straightedge" movement: youth who discipline their bodies, do not use drugs or alcohol, stay away from sex, and keep themselves physically fit. Often parents are pleased with the newfound structure in the lives of their teens but are not aware that the glue holding this group together is an extreme antigovernment attitude. The self-discipline they pursue and parade is not intended to honor God, but rather is a means to survive the future conflict they think is inevitable.

Learning about this trend sharpened my preaching. Rather than urging young Christians to be disciplined, I now say that self-discipline for its own sake is not enough. I say that the reason we discipline ourselves is for the glory of God. Not only is it more relevant to youth but it is closer to the biblical ethic of self-discipline.

The relevance of passion

When I was younger I worried a time would come when I no longer would be able to communicate well, that my ideas would eventually grow out-of-date. I no longer fear that. Although I work diligently to stay current, I am learning that being out-of-date has less to do with age and more to do with being authentic in character, wholesome in attitude, and disciplined in study. Preaching is communicating relevant godly information in a package that can be understood by the hearer. But preaching must be presented through a person who has a genuine walk with God. The gentleman who was the interim pastor just prior to my coming to the church I now serve is an outstanding communicator. People of all ages connected with his sermons. With a natural sense of humor, he addressed even the most serious issues. But more important, the congregation sensed his heart for God. One reason some ministers lose their power in the pulpit in mid-life is that they have lost their passion. The exegesis may be accurate, the logic unflawed, and the language like that of a poet, but unless there is spiritual passion the material is out-of-date because the preacher's soul is not up-to-date.

In early 1987 I felt as though my spiritual life was in a fog. It was a difficult stretch of life for me for a variety of reasons. Simply to survive, I preached old sermons I had delivered at another church. I tried to add enough current information, with an illustration upgrade here and there, so no one would know.

About the time the fog seemed to be lifting, I delivered a new, never-before-preached sermon. A member complimented me: "You preached today like you really believed it."

"I hope I always do."

He countered, "Sometimes you preach as though you think we ought to believe it, such as the way I talk to my children about eating balanced meals. They know I believe it, but they also know it is not too important in my own life."

More than staying in touch with the younger generation, I want to preach with spiritual passion. I want to preach as though I believe the gospel, for at mid-life I truly believe it more than ever.

7

THE NEXT LEVEL

I ONCE PREACHED ON THE "Do not provoke your children to wrath" passage from Ephesians 6:4. I approached it from the perspective of a thirty-two-year-old dad of three preschoolers—that's what I was—struggling to find the line between discipline and punishment. I was convinced I had thoroughly exegeted the text before I began preparing my sermon.

I recently revisited the same text while preaching a series from the book of Ephesians. I pulled my study notes from my files and was startled to see how much of my life experiences as a thirty-two-year-old not only influenced my sermon content and illustrations but my exegetical research as well. I found I could not dip into my old notes and simply review discoveries I had made in a previous exploration. I was now fifty, the father of three adult daughters. I found one commentary particularly helpful this time as I studied the passage, the same commentary I looked at all those years ago but from which I chose to use almost no material. Not only was I bringing my immediate experiences to bear on the text but the passage raised different questions for me, issues I never would have considered twenty years ago.

For example, what does this text say to a sixty-year-old gentleman who is dealing with guilt now because he was so afraid of "provoking his children to wrath" when they were young that he never confronted them appropriately? This gentleman so much wanted to be kind that he allowed his children to make wrong choices, and now he lives with the consequences. He has also resorted to correcting his adult children in such a way that they are angry with him.

In short, if I had not dug new footings for my sermons on Ephesians—and instead built my sermons on what notes I had created many years ago—I would never have dealt with the key issues facing my congregation.

I want to continue in this chapter the theme of staying fresh in our preaching, but here I want to focus on the sermon-preparation process. Mid-life can bring sweetness to the task of preparing for Sunday mornings. We have worked through much of the Bible by now, and our life-experience aids us in the task of applying God's Word in a way that rings true with real life. While a phalanx of temptations confronts the sermon-preparation process, new disciplines have helped me take new ground as I try to raise the level of my preaching in the second half of life.

Airbrush enemy

A minister who in some ways has been my mentor taught me about the continuing task of study. In his early sixties, he is a gifted communicator. I like to hear him preach because he not only has outstanding content, he speaks with power and passion. It is evident that he prepares well. His illustrations are current, and he avoids clichés.

Curious about what goes on behind the scenes, I spent a day with him to see how he worked. The biggest takeaway from my time with him was his simple declaration that he had made a conscious decision not to rely on his past material.

He said there are at least two enemies to sermon preparation for the experienced minister. The first is not the exclusive foe of mature preachers, but is a common opponent for all generations of preachers: fighting the battle for adequate preparation time, regardless of age. The second enemy, though, rarely attacks the preaching novice. An experienced preacher has so much material accumulated in his mind and in his files, he knows he can create a sermon without opening a book and doing fresh research. By pulling out old files and skimming previous research, the minister can quickly prepare a twenty-minute sermon. It is even easier if the preacher has kept manuscripts; with a few minor tweaks and verbal airbrush strokes, *voilà!*

The familiarity of the Bible can also tempt us to neglect new exegesis. When I was young, I felt pressure to perform on Sunday mornings, because preaching is considered one of the primary tasks of the minister. I made sure I carved out the time for preparation. Now at midlife, after nearly thirty years of studying God's Word, I can accomplish even new exegesis more quickly than I could at age twenty-three. But I often wonder, *Am I taking less time because I am more efficient at preparation? Or am I just more involved with other things?*

After talking with numerous pastors, I have concluded that pastors who did not keep their preaching fresh knew deep down they were cheating and that seemed to affect their attitude. They were more cynical, which affected their entire view of ministry. Conversely, pastors who stayed fresh in their preaching felt good about the rest of pastoral work. Every time I hang around with the sixty-two-year-old pastor I mentioned at the beginning of this section, I get jazzed about preaching. I love hearing the excitement in his voice as he speaks about his study. Every time I am around him I find I want to do better preaching and be a better minister.

In addition to familiarity with the Word, another enemy of preparation in mid-life can be our current interests or life theme. Some pastors, rather than becoming complacent in their study, tend to focus too exclusively on one area of interest as they get older. It shows up in their preaching, and congregations may become bored hearing the same issue over and over. One church recently terminated its pastor for several reasons, but at least one of them was his Johnny-one-note preaching. He was a good person and a decent-enough preacher, but his interest in eschatology led him to become an expert on the subject. He preached on it repeatedly and found ways to work it into almost every sermon. His people agreed with his conclusions for the most part but they wearied of the topic. He left feeling the church did not see the need for eschatology; the church is determined to avoid any preacher who broaches the subject. If a candidate for their pulpit makes the mistake of preaching from the book of Daniel, he will not likely survive the lions' den.

While the above illustration may be glaring, it is natural for us to focus on what we know well or what God has brought to our attention through the years—our life theme. One way I am trying to guard against hammering away at only one theme is by starting my sermon evaluation process after I have prepared my sermon and before I have delivered it. Too often Monday has been my primary day of reflection. But now I try to discipline myself to ask, "Am I addressing this issue every week in one form or another?" or "Is there too much of me in the message?"

One Saturday night I eliminated an entire section of a sermon because I realized I had addressed the issue of money—in different ways—on each of the previous five Sundays. After some reflection, I concluded money was the issue I was personally facing at the time. I had been preaching to a felt need all right—my own. Although we must be sensitive to the leadership of the Holy Spirit, we must also be aware that often the voice of the Holy Spirit can sound a lot like our own voice. To preach only from our interests or hurts is to abuse the place God has given us and to take advantage of the pulpit the church has allowed us to fill.

A friend recently realized that for much of his ministry, he had ignored the Old Testament prophets. He began a thorough study and now preaches from them quite often. He says this has helped his preaching in other areas but that he must work to guard against using his sermons as a place to display his new appreciation of the prophets. Soon after I turned forty-five, I realized I rarely preached from the Psalms except at funerals and other sad occasions. I had used the Psalms as words to comfort the bereaved but never as words for celebration.

A final remark about the enemies of effective preaching at mid-life: by this point we know what we can get away with. We know how to fill a twenty-two-minute time slot with twelve minutes of material (preaching expands to fill the time allotted for it). The temptation is to do that every week. Some time ago we had a guest preacher for a special event at our church, and he obviously had not done his preparation. He had one story, which he told extremely well, but he preached for twenty-five minutes, and the entire sermon revolved around that one story. While the congregation was attentive, several people later said to me, "He didn't have much substance. He had only one story." Yet from my perspective, most of the congregation were complimentary to him. I am sure he left our church feeling he had preached well.

And perhaps that is the most scary aspect of preaching at any age: few people will tell us the truth, and when some do, we may dismiss them as cranks. For our preaching to be better in the second half of life than it was in the first demands new disciplines; it demands that we tighten down the preparation process.

Beginning with the new

For my current Sunday morning preparation, I have come up with some new techniques, changes in the way I approach the study of God's Word. First I make a conscious decision to read new sources. When preaching a series on 1 Corinthians, for example, I read the epistle in a different Bible translation—one I had never studied before. The unfamiliar translation gave me a different slant on the text. I also consulted new commentaries, and only after the new research did I refer to my old reliable books and old material.

This may sound like a time-consuming process, but one of the advantages of experience in study is that I can skim an author's work quickly and catch the drift as well as his biases. I am also more aware of my blind spots, things I missed in a text when I was younger.

I have also begun dating my files. I have three files on prayer now instead of one. The last is labeled "Prayer 1995." I know everything in that folder will have been placed there after January 1, 1995. This small change in my filing system prevents my using outdated illustrations. Recently while preaching a series on prayer, I used notes from three different periods of research. In going through my old files, I found more of the material was illustration-oriented, while much of the recent material was more application-directed. Once again I was reminded of the importance of creating fresh material and not relying solely on previous study.

Today I often wait to write my sermon until Thursday and Friday. When I was younger, I began the research and writing on Monday and Tuesday because I was afraid I would not have enough material to develop a twenty-five-minute sermon. While I still research the text on Monday and Tuesday, I may not write the actual sermon until later in the week. Now I have so many more sources that I have more of a sense of what I need to pull in; I am confident I will have enough to say, but I want to make sure I have the *right* thing to say.

I probably devote more time to oral preparation than I used to. It has always been true to a degree that what communicates in writing does not necessarily come across as well when it is spoken, but we live in an increasingly oral, emotive, nonlinear culture. It is even more critical to prepare orally before giving the sermon. Sermons that sound like research papers will not be listened to, much less understood. Many college students are now required to prepare some research papers using PowerPoint software, which is designed for the visual-oriented reader.

Not long ago, after I preached in our early Sunday service, I realized the first two sentences of my sermon sounded like the opening lines of a bad novel. So between services I went into my study and reworked the opening—not rewriting it, but speaking it aloud. I was saying essentially the same thing, but I conveyed it in a much fresher way. Usually I don't wait until *after* I have preached to polish the oral presentation. Rather, I have learned to integrate my oral and written preparation: I write a passage, then speak it out loud; rewrite a paragraph, and speak it again. I recently preached on the Psalms in our Wednesday night service, and I came across a wonderful line about Psalm 12 in Eugene Peterson's *Leap Over a Wall*. It described the heart of that passage as well as anything I have ever read. Then I read it aloud and realized it did not communicate orally. Even as I was speaking the sentence, it felt awkward. As recently as ten years ago I would not have caught that and would have quoted it verbatim and added the appropriate footnote. But this time I put the phrase in my own words, while giving credit to Peterson.

On the fly

One skill that gets better with age is the ability to read your congregation while preaching. I can sense when I am connecting with people and when I am not, and I adjust accordingly. When I was younger, I often had no clue as to whether or not my preaching was connecting with the congregation. Only if people went to sleep or walked out did I catch on that I had missed the target. Later, I could pick up on body language to determine when I was not connecting—no direct eye contact, restlessness, shuffling of bulletins—but all I knew to do was raise my voice or increase the intensity, thinking that would drive home my point.

I now look at four or five people in the congregation

and take direction from them. One woman sits in the fourth row, and I have learned that when she is not quite getting it, she gets a different look on her face. One fellow sits in the center section and avoids eye contact with me when I have either missed his head or his heart. I also listen for the general rustling and shuffling of feet that signals the congregation is bored or confused.

Clyde Fant, who was probably one of the most effective teachers of preachers of the last forty years in Southern Baptist circles, once told me, "If you preach a sermon word for word the way you wrote it, you probably haven't brought out your best." He said we need to learn to trust those ideas or phrases that occur to us during our preaching.

Once I was speaking on futility from a Christian perspective and how we don't often see immediate results. I came up with a line during the message: "It doesn't do any good to do any good." It was an ordinary sermon, but I decided to use that line as a refrain throughout, and it drove home one of the key ideas of the sermon in a powerful, memorable way.

Preaching is a God-called and congregation-allowed privilege. We must resist the pride that can creep into how we view our own preaching and that can cripple our effectiveness. Until we receive our first retirement check, we can never give in to the entropy inherent in the task of preaching God's Word. We must always think of ourselves as novices. And as a novice, my best preaching may be yet to come.

8

WITH A LITTLE HELP FROM MY FRIENDS

WHEN THE SEARCH COMMITTEE at my current church was considering my qualifications, they interviewed some parishioners at my former church. The committee was glad to hear that I was close to everyone equally and did not play favorites. Although the committee viewed this as a compliment, I am not sure it was. It merely said that I had mastered the illusion of intimacy. For some reasons I will probably never know, I was closer to fewer people there than I had been at any other church.

This phenomenon has been discussed at length in ministry publications such as LEADERSHIP JOURNAL and others, but the truth is even more painful at mid-life: although we have relationships with many in the church, we may be close to no one. This is compounded by the fact that most every person in the church feels as if he or she knows the pastor on some level. Many of us, by our use of personal illustrations in sermons, may give others the feeling that they know us personally. They do not. Some pastors, especially from my generation and older, may even have denied themselves close personal friendships in the church out of fear of being cliquish.

Now past fifty, I no longer want to be a mile wide and an inch deep in the sea of relationships. I have recognized the importance of having a few deep friendships because I find they make me an emotionally healthier person and thus a better pastor. When I talk with other ministers my age, I hear that the lack of real friendship is a common issue. I know a few pastors who have given up the illusion of intimacy that several shallow relationships create and have said, in effect, "I don't care if I make somebody angry or that a minister is supposed to be friends with everyone. I need close friends." Not only is having friends good for pastors but admitting the need for them is often as therapeutic as the relationships themselves.

I began to feel this thirst for deep friendships when I was in my forties. Earlier, I was too ambitious and goal-oriented to give priority to relationships. As time went on, however, I began to make a few close friends both inside and outside the church. The need for close friendships was driven home to me when a church acquaintance, about four years older than me, came to visit. I asked him how things were going.

"I'm lonely," he said. "Basically, if I died now I don't know who would be my pallbearers. I have business associates and family members, but . . . ."

That was painful to hear. I thought about my friends: the truth is, if I have no one to carry my body when I die, it probably means no one is carrying me while I am alive. I sensed he was telling my story as well as his own. Since then, I have made more of a conscious effort to develop good friendships.

As we head into the mid- to late summer of life, earthly friendships, in addition to our friendship with God, are key to a life of fullness. Friendships may be something we never had much time for after college. But now our kids are grown and gone—or almost gone—and ostensibly we have more time. One way to fill that extra time is to invest it getting to know people more intimately. Throughout this book I warn about the temptation to decelerate from pastoral work in mid-life. That is not what I am advocating here. I am simply saying that healthy friendships are critical to making the second half of life better than the first.

Friendship barriers

Contrary to conventional wisdom, I am not sure ministers are any lonelier than any other segment of adults. Loneliness is a society-wide problem. I read once that lawyers and physicians think their professions are the most susceptible to loneliness. Pastors may face some unique obstacles to building friendships, but these are by no means insurmountable.

One barrier I struggle to clear is a natural suspicion of people who seem to want to be friends with me, particularly when I start a new pastorate. Someone once said, "Be careful of the person who meets you at the airport when you first arrive in town, offering to carry your luggage, because if you're not careful, you will soon be carrying *their* bags." Bruce Grubbs, who has written on the subject of moving to a new pastorate, says the first few people who come to you may be "stalking horses" for the rest of the congregation. They may come with a personal problem, but everyone else is watching to see how the new pastor handles it. I have found both of these scenarios to be accurate to some extent. The negative for the pastor is that such knowledge can lead to cynicism, which erects barriers to friendship. We may react guardedly when someone seems to make overtures of friendship. The real fear is of being "owned" by someone. But if we allow this fear to dominate us, we risk becoming loners.

Other barriers come through people's perceptions of ministers. We generally interact with people for only short periods of time. Someone pops into our study with a quick question; we exchange a few words with some after church; we attend Sunday school functions once or twice a year and mingle; we take part in a parishioner's daughter's or son's wedding. It is easy to fall into a pattern, therefore, of talking only about surface issues. As a result, some people may think there isn't much substance to pastors, so they may treat pastors like an encyclopedia—something no one reads all the way through or for any length of time.

Part of this may be our own fault. We pastors do not always know how to ask good questions, and asking good questions is one door to friendship. Part of our calling is to *answer* questions people have, so we may not be sensitive to the fact that someone may simply want to chat about his or her own experiences.

Recently, after our midweek service, someone asked me four questions about my time at a conference I had attended in the Silicon Valley. His questions guided our entire conversation. It was not until I got into my car that I realized he had told me that he too had just been to a conference in the same part of the country. I did not have the vaguest idea why he was there because I had not asked him. Instead, I talked about my trip as if I were reporting on how I had spent my time there as his pastor. I thought we were connecting because I was answering his questions, but he had no doubt been waiting to tell me his story. His questions were his way of saying, "I'd like to tell you why I was out there." I missed an opportunity to ask about something that was probably vitally important to him.

I am sure he thought, *What a bore!*

We pastors may appear boring to others outside our profession, but not because of the profession itself. The nature of church work can be all-consuming; too many of us talk only about church. This is probably because too many of us have no life outside the church, and therefore it can be hard to find points of commonality with other people.

Don't rescue me

The time to nurture friendships is not during pain. Rarely have I made a lasting friendship with someone when I was really hurting. Once while undergoing some intense criticism, I felt sorry for myself and thought I needed someone with whom I could talk. A guy came up to me and said, essentially, "Hey, I've admired you from a distance. I think we think alike. Let me be your friend." I was vulnerable—and I got taken. Things I told him in confidence came back to haunt me. I spent the next several months retrieving bits and pieces of information from people who had been hurt by the information he had divulged.

During a tough stretch of church work, we can bottle up our emotions and be tempted to vent to the first person who reaches out in friendship. The danger is that we may end up a victim or worse yet victimize someone else by drawing them close for the wrong reasons.

For troubled pastors, friends outside the church are usually better listeners or at least can provide more accurate and less biased feedback, since they do not have to filter everything through your role as their pastor. Professional counselors can also assist. A friend of mine has a quarterly checkup with a counselor. He discovered he can allow anger to build to the boiling point and then let it overflow into his most personal relationships. I am fortunate to have a psychiatrist friend with whom I meet every other month. The questions he asks me help me to stay in touch with my feelings. Our friendship developed after he heard me speak at a civic club meeting and dropped me a note gently disagreeing with some of my conclusions. I followed up on his comments and we have been talking ever since.

I spoke at a deacons' retreat at a church in a different

part of the state, and in my talk I quoted something from *Wired* magazine. A gentleman approached me afterward and said, "You read the same magazine I read." We started chatting, and I liked him immediately. Some time later, he and his wife moved to our city and joined our church. My wife and I both sensed we had a lot in common with them, so we set out to develop a friendship. We liked them and invited them over. It was as simple as that.

The only other alternative is to sit at home feeling sorry for ourselves. Two mid-life ministers told me virtually the same story—that they had experienced a breakthrough in friendships when they accepted responsibility for their own loneliness. I mentioned in a previous chapter the importance of taking responsibility for our spirituality. The same applies in the area of friendships. It's easy to drink deeply from the well of self-pity and assume that no one will be our friend because we are ministers. Often people think we are too busy, so they don't invite us over for that reason. The way to combat this misconception is to invite them over to our house. I have never regretted taking the initiative in friendship, although not every contact worked out to be a lasting friendship. I do regret not always taking the opportunity to ask someone to lunch or a ball game.

The deep and true friendships are those we make one on one, over time. I understand the value of accountability groups, but these do not necessarily provide deep relationships. In accountability groups, men are usually seeking information for a specific purpose, and most come with the attitude, "Let's get him through this and headed in the right direction."

I have seen ministers' groups that seek to provide both accountability and friendship, but they tend to break down. Within the profession, it can be difficult to make friends with others because there is a subtle temptation to rank other ministers as our teachers, our peers, or our students. In general, friendships with other ministers can be fragile. A sense of competition—woven into the fabric of a male soul—often steers us away from each other. This is unfortunate, because it has kept people on the same team from building relationships. And competition does not necessarily diminish with age. It is a spiritual issue directly related to pride. Confessing it and experiencing genuine humility does not only make us better ministers but opens the doors to friendships.

Also, because so many younger ministers move frequently, some may think, *Why should I get to know another minister? He'll only be moving away soon.* By mid-life, career moves often slow down, and sometimes the doors to friendships with those in our religious neighborhood may be more open.

The key point is this: The best kinds of friendship are those that are more relaxed, fuller, less structured than relationships that develop in accountability groups or ministerial groups. The purpose should be the relationship itself, and not common issues that bind us together.

One for the road ahead

Recently I visited with a man who has truly finished well in ministry. Now in his late sixties, he is often sought after as a pulpit guest and interim minister. He described to me a younger man who, through moral improprieties, lost his church and probably will never pastor again. My friend said of the younger minister, "I watched him first disconnect from his friends, then his wife, and eventually his children. Somewhere along the way he became emotionally disconnected from God. But I have learned that no one stays disconnected from everyone. Ministry is allowing your connection with God to guide you in all other connections."

Ministry is a life of connections. We are connected to God, to our family, to our church family, and to our friends. Often the desire to escape results in a disconnectedness in one or all of these areas. To stay connected, we need to consciously choose to keep in touch regularly with these relationships.

I have been blessed with a few close friendships. One began in my early thirties, shortly after I suffered an embarrassing incident at the church I was pastoring. I was moderating a business meeting, when I literally passed out. It was assumed it was due to stress, but at my age I was not about to admit to that. I worried about being perceived as weak. As it turned out, I had picked up a virus while on vacation. On my first Sunday back after recovering, I felt as if I had to explain myself continually: "No, I am not under stress, I had a virus." I am quite sure the church got tired of hearing this.

I also visited a couple that were in our church on that first Sunday back. My contact was routine; I simply encouraged them to worship with us again. The fellow and I connected. I cannot explain beyond that how the relationship took off. Looking back, I think he may have been the only person I visited that week to whom I felt I did not have to explain my fainting fiasco, but in the weeks to come our friendship developed, and our wives became close friends, too.

That particular friendship opened some new areas in our lives. I have never been much of a golfer but I golf because he golfs. He is not a big basketball fan but he goes to games with me. We have been friends for eighteen years, and that through several moves. We keep up with each other's lives, calling about every major career decision we make. His geographical distance from me has actually been helpful because he can be objective about a situation. He asks me questions I may not even know to ask myself and helps me without ever giving advice. Because he is not an accountability partner, he is not judging me or checking up on my integrity. He is just my friend. Recently we were together again and the conversation strengthened my soul. Yet our meetings do not contain the "didja" language. Did you read your Bible? Did you pray? Did you have impure thoughts?

Instead, we tell about our journey. Accountability groups keep us holy. Friends keep us sane. I need more sanity in the second half of life.

9

GRACE AT HOME

I HATE HARRY CHAPIN'S popular folk tune of the mid-seventies, "Cat's in the Cradle." In case you are not familiar with it, it is about a father who reflects on how when his son was small he never took time to play with him because he was too busy. Well, the son grows up and because of his job and family he does not have time for his father. The grown son ends a phone call with: "It's sure been nice talking to you." The father realizes then that his son has become just like he was.

The message is poignant: what goes around comes around. If we are too busy for our kids while they are young, someday they will be too busy for us. And that is why I hate the song. Perhaps I feel a little guilty, now that my daughters are grown. Many pastors struggle to spend adequate time with their children. Although we have always known that our family needed to be a priority, the consequences always seemed so far away. But not so at mid-life.

I have a friend who feels so guilty about the time he missed with his children when they were small that now he is overcompensating. His well-intentioned penance is creating tension in the family. By attempting to be their

131

buddy, he has relinquished his role as their middle-aged father. One of his children told me that his father wants so much time with him when he comes home that he dreads coming. They are in college, they have their own lives, and their response to him is something like, "Face it, Dad, we're too old to play catch in the yard. We're adults now."

No matter how hard we try, we cannot make up for the amount of time we *did not* spend with our children. That can be difficult to accept. Our generation has probably preached more on the subject of family than the two generations of preachers before us combined. And, frankly, most of us have likely preached far better messages on the subject of family than we have lived. At least that is true of me.

My greatest regret is not that I wasn't at home enough. My greatest regret is that *when* I was at home I was not at home. I was not emotionally available for my family. I did not connect with them. Even though I left the office and came home, I rarely left the church mentally. In that sense, I was not present for my children. Shortly after we had moved to a new church, I was working diligently to help revitalize an aging church by starting some innovative programs. The result was little time at home and emotional disconnectedness with my kids even when I was home.

"Dad, is this church too big for you?" one of my daughters asked. Her question both angered and threatened me, as if she were questioning my competence, but I knew what she was really saying was, "My life is hurt-

ing as a result of your having this church."

A few minutes later I sat down with her and said, "I don't know. It could be too big."

When I asked her why she asked the question, she said, "You're never at home. And when you are, you're always in such a bad mood."

Another time, a key family decision was made without me. I asked my wife why I had not been consulted. "You're never home enough to ask," she said. After I explained to her why I had been so busy at church and recited from memory three pages from my Day-Timer, she said, "To be honest, I didn't know if you would even be interested in this issue." And she was right. I probably wasn't. But my feelings were hurt because I was not asked.

Mid-life naturally brings some regret: about career, about past choices, about family. But at some point we must begin to live in the present. We cannot rewind the clock. We are here, at this time, at this moment, and no matter what type of parent or spouse we have been up to this point, our family needs us *now*. Just as pastors need to reinvent their approach to work at middle age, we may need to reinvent our approach to family.

No longer needed

When we reach mid-life, our children are either teenagers or grown adults who do not need us in the same way as they did when they were younger; our relationship with them has changed or is changing. Spouses who stayed home during the nesting years return to careers or develop interests that may or may not be related to the church. That can bring a new set of issues for the mid-life pastor: with the current emphasis on family in the Christian community, churches like having a pastor who has children living at home. Although most search committees and church boards would probably not admit it, there may even be a bias against childless couples and empty-nest couples. A pastor with a spouse and children at home makes the church appear to be a family church. The pastor's family often becomes the projected self-image of the church. What is ironic is that churches want a pastor with a big family at home but want him to work as if he had taken the vow of celibacy.

But we cannot blame the church entirely for the pressures. Often the blame lies deep within the soul of the pastor who is motivated by insecurity and guilt rather than by his call and by grace. The same issues that keep us from being good family members in our early years can keep us from being good family members in our middle years. Although impossible to start over, mid-course corrections are possible. Time demands placed on us by our children are less, and though this can be emotionally difficult to handle, it can also be the opportunity for a new beginning.

There may be, however, at least one unique issue for pastors to face at mid-life. Many of us thrive on being needed. If your self-worth gauge hits the full mark only when you are told, "We don't know how we could make it without you," you will have difficulty when your children or spouse become more independent. Some deal with this by assuming the role of the "father of the church," which usually means becoming over-involved at church.

I know a man who is on staff at a large church. When his last child graduated from high school, the congregation became concerned that he was spending so much time at work that, ironically, he was getting in the way of the work of the church. This pastor had struggled with many of the typical parenting issues as a young father but had made some adjustments and improved his relationship with his children. During this stage he also became a better minister and church employee because he had learned to delegate and empower others to do their ministry. Nevertheless, after his children left home he began to use his extra time to micro-manage his responsibilities at church, effectively keeping others from their work. His wife's career was also blossoming, and he felt unneeded. Rather than adapt to the changes, he shifted the focus of his parenting skills to the church and, arguably, attempted to father the church.

He never seemed to get down to the real issue at work in his soul: his need to be needed by others in order to have a sense of his own worth and value. Instead of pouring himself into the church, it would have been more beneficial to all if he would have taken the "lonely road" and begun the hard work of reflecting on his motivations.

Other pastors may tend to back away from their grown children at mid-life, declaring in effect that their role as a parent is over. That rationale may be an attempt to avoid the guilt of past failures. Others may be so intent on being free from parental responsibilities that they abdicate the role.

I meet occasionally with the adult children of a minister, and once they asked me how to go about rebuilding a relationship with their father. Although he had been an adequate father during their years at home, he was now acting as though his children were adults but not his adult children. He had essentially severed his emotional ties with them. He told them, "I haven't done anything wrong; you are adults. If we are close that is fine, if we are not close that is also fine." His children resented the fact that he seemed happier at the moment than at any time in their lives.

In less than two years he resigned his church, telling the congregation he was too tired to care anymore, that he was wrung out from ministry. That event, coupled with how he had responded to his children, indicated to me an issue of the soul.

I cannot speculate about the noise level inside his head, but with the advent of mid-life, I personally had to face the painful truth that as a parent of adult children, I am a mere mortal. The simple equation that young people have children at home and I do not have children at home, therefore I am not young anymore, is enough to cause a dark night of the soul.

From coach to cheerleader

Where do we go with these feelings? How can we redefine our roles as parent and spouse?

My wife and I were in a somber, reflective mood driving to our daughter's college graduation. It was a bittersweet time for us. I began reflecting on how poor a father I had been and how I wished I could take back those lost years. My wife had some regrets, too, but she pointed out that if we kept up the melancholy conversation, neither of us would be able to enjoy this special occasion in our daughter's life.

My wife helped me to see that we still have some significant contributions to make in the lives of our three adult daughters. That is, we are still their parents; we have a role to fill. God willing, I have another twenty years or more to be their father. It will not be the same role but it can be just as satisfying.

For example, I can be a sounding board for them as they make choices about college, careers, and marriage. But I am learning that my new role is not so much a coach as it is a cheerleader. The coaching role of a younger father hopefully prepares his children to coach themselves as they mature. One key step in making this transition is to move from being someone who gives advice to someone who asks questions. Recently my youngest daughter changed her major at college. We had a wonderful conversation about this change. I resisted the temptation to probe her for information only for my benefit, such as "How many more years of college will this mean?" Instead, I asked questions that helped her to see the implications of her options—*and* I was able to listen to her feelings. I sensed she was not asking for my approval so much as my blessing. To give our blessing is to honor the decisions of our adult children. They have listened to our lectures on life for many years. Now it is time for them to make choices and live with the consequences. They need to coach themselves, and I need to be their cheerleader.

I am also trying to rethink my role with my wife. Since our kids have grown, Alta Faye has been redefining herself and her role in the family. In the ministry, the wife of a pastor is viewed as the minister's wife, the mother of his children, the church's servant, and co-laborer with her husband. Although our spouses fill these roles, it is easy to ignore the most important truth about them: they are individuals. It was a major transition in our marriage when I saw my wife redefine her life. She took motherhood very seriously, and I was concerned that when the kids moved out she might struggle to find her identity. My worries were unfounded.

She has never felt that teaching the Bible is one of her spiritual gifts, but she recently decided to participate in the leadership of our Wednesday and Sunday teaching ministries. She saw a need and decided to explore her gifts. And though I never thought of my wife as a civic-minded person, she has begun to pursue civic and community activities. She has also begun to mentor some of the young mothers in our church.

In short, she has not waited for someone to redefine her role or to prod her in that direction. Rather, she has quietly taken the initiative. Lyle Schaller, a prolific writer and church consultant, once said, "If you ask a church who are the most competent people within the body, the list will be made up of women in their fifties."

Although I do not understand all the reasons for it, mid-life appears to be a wonderful occasion for women to realize their dreams. Certainly one reason is that they now have the time and energy to pursue new avenues. We need to release them for that adventure. It is sometimes said that such-and-such a pastor would be a better minister if his wife were more supportive. It works both ways. The pastor's wife may be a better Christian if her husband is more supportive of her. The willingness to support our wives in their dreams is one of the keys to success and happiness at mid-life.

A friend in the ministry recently confided to me the effect of his wife's volunteer work in their church. Although she does not teach or assume a role of leadership, her career has assumed various roles as a volunteer. My friend admitted that earlier in his ministry he somewhat resented his wife's work in the church. Now at mid-life he has come to see it as valid as his own. He even feels that her work may have affected more people for the sake of the kingdom than his paid duties as a church staff member.

Recently a psychologist told me that young pastors and young coaches have much in common. Both are intent on winning and both often carry the competitive spirit home. Wives of coaches and wives of ministers often sit in the stands or the pews and watch their husbands perform and then listen to the remarks of the fans or the congregation. Mid-life is the time for a reversal of that scenario.

A time to heal

Some ministers and their spouses have endured great amounts of pain because of the behavior of their children—wandering prodigals who have made wrong choices and maybe even estranged themselves from their families. When these ministry families hit the half-century mark in age, they often want to quit, believing they are unworthy to continue in the ministry.

I have a colleague whose children made unhealthy lifestyle choices, and this pastor and his wife have for several years carried the heavy burden of guilt: "If only we had done this or that differently. . . ." But he came to realize that he was not responsible for his children's conduct. His responsibility was to teach them when they were young. With the help of some friends and a mental-health professional, he was able to admit that although he and his wife had not been perfect parents, they had not been bad parents. Many of us knew they had provided a solid foundation for their children— upon which their children had simply decided not to build. Rather than beat himself up emotionally, he chose to place the ultimate responsibility on the shoulders of his children.

By the same token, many of us whose children have brought us joy must be careful not to congratulate ourselves for the actions of our offspring. The first step toward a healthy attitude about family is to realize that we are only responsible for what we put into our children, not for how they turn out. Perhaps this concept is easier to accept and apply when it relates to the church family. A minister can proclaim the gospel clearly, serve with integrity, care for his people with genuine love—and still see spiritual or moral failure in his or her church. The minister cannot accept responsibility for the personal failures of his congregation. The apostle Paul was not the reason for the problems at the church at Corinth, even though he was its founding pastor. Paul invested in the church at Corinth, and despite all his efforts it was a divided church, there was immorality, and there was abuse of the Lord's Supper.

But Paul did not walk away from the church wringing his hands and saying, "Where did I go wrong?" Instead of writing a letter detailing his failures, he addressed their issues.

I am not trying to excuse poor parenting. I am merely pointing out that bad things can happen to good parents. The first step toward healing in a family is forgiveness. Loving parents must forgive children who have failed. And parents who feel they have failed must come to the place over time where they can receive forgiveness from their heavenly Father. Some parents are so wounded by the behavior of their children that they neglect to work on what they are responsible for: their relationship with the heavenly Father.

A friend who made some tragic moral choices that hurt his family and resulted in the loss of his position in a large Christian organization was asked to speak to a group of younger ministers in a retreat setting. In his address he said, "Some of you are probably questioning whether I ought to be here speaking to you, as well as wondering how I can live with myself knowing the hurt I have caused my family. The answer to those concerns is found in the sermons you preach each week: it is *grace!* What keeps me sane is knowing that even though I am responsible for a great amount of hurt, God still loves me. The major difference between the fellow that once climbed the ministerial ladder and myself is that now I know God loves me because of grace. Much of my ministry I preached grace but really believed God loved me because I was good."

We can't go back. There are no second chances. It seems obvious, but it is the only point at which we can make marriage and family all that it was meant to be in the second half of life. We can celebrate the family we have and determine to mend the hurts and rebuild. Midlife is not beginning again, but rather a time for adjustment. We will never be able to make up for the nights we should have been home or for the times we were home but our hearts and minds were at the church.

Our families still need us, even though they do not need the father or mother they should have had twenty years ago. Our spouses need us more than ever, but they do not need us to be the partners we weren't twenty years ago. An older minister once told me, "When you are young in the ministry, you find joy when your members do right. When you grow older, you find joy when your members find grace."

The middle adult years are good when we discover grace for our families and grace for ourselves.

10

WELL WITH MY SOUL

WHEN I WAS THIRTY-FIVE, I was asked to be host for a well-known preacher who was the featured guest at a conference. My job was to transport him to and from his speaking engagements. During one session of the conference, this "pulpit prince" said that most ministers he knew lived with a deep sense of desperation.

That statement did not square with what I knew of my acquaintances and friends who were pastors. Was he simply using hyperbole?

Later, when we were in the car together, I asked him to elaborate on his comment. As I listened intently, it became clear to me that desperation was a factor not only in the lives of his friends but occasionally visited his own soul as well. At the time, I simply could not grasp the concept of desperation, much less why someone of his stature would struggle with it.

I do now.

He was nearly fifty years old, and, without intending to, he summed up the spiritual plight of the middle-aged pastor—loneliness of soul.

Mid-life can bring a string of losses, and these can trigger loneliness. It can seem as though all our dependable supports, the foundations upon which we have come to count, are knocked out from under us. We lose the youthful energy that allowed us to stay up all night to prepare for a major presentation and still appear fresh the next day. Our body does not bounce back the way it used to, and we can no longer cover our lack of preparation with youthful passion. An overly enthusiastic fifty-two-year-old can come across as an aging vacuum cleaner salesman.

Nor can we rely on family the way we used to. When we arrive home in the evening, the kids are either out or busy with their own interests. Our spouse has a life of her own, too. And the congregation that supports a young pastor ("He's new at this, he's going to make a few mistakes") may be less tolerant of a middle-aged veteran. More subtly, we realize we cannot count on being able to figure everything out. A younger pastor may struggle with the issues of his calling, but he assumes deep down that with time and experience he will be able to correct his mistakes. Years ago, even when I felt discouraged, I was still confident that with more time and more work I could remove the source of the discouragement. I firmly believed that *someday* I would get it right.

By fifty, I realized there were some things I would never get right, some problems I would never solve. That, among other things, created within me a sense of desperation—the same desperation described by the well-known preacher at the beginning of this chapter.

A retired pastor who served the same congregation

for thirty years told me of a defining moment in his ministry. When he was forty-two, a woman in his church was angry with him over a decision he had made regarding vacation Bible school. At the height of her emotional outburst, she said, "I will still be here when you are gone!"

He smiled, knowing he planned to stay and she was at least fifteen years older than him.

She was still working in the vacation Bible school program when he turned fifty-four, and he remembered their conversation. He sensed she was still angry with him, even though he had performed her daughter's wedding and officiated at her husband's funeral.

He told me it was at that point that he realized he could not spend the rest of his ministry trying to fix what was broken. The woman was present at his retirement reception and her feelings for him had never changed.

These types of situations are what contribute to loneliness of the soul, which in turn can create a kind of quiet desperation that can dog us for years. A few pastors who are not able to cope with this, deal with their loneliness in a way that destroys their family and their calling.

Loneliness can be a spiritual issue that plays itself out in tangible ways. An older minister once told me that sexual drive does not necessarily decrease in middle age but common sense often does. Some lose their place of service because of inappropriate conduct in interpersonal relationships. In previous chapters I have focused on calling and character. Here, I would like to explore our relationship with God and how the desperation of mid-life can be an opportunity for spiritual renewal, for creating a new hunger for God and for writing a new chapter in our lives.

Taking ownership

There comes a time when a Christian leader realizes that he or she must take responsibility for his or her own spiritual development. While ostensibly this should have occurred years earlier, it is easy to operate parasitically off the spiritual life of others, and so this revelation may not come until mid-life.

Paradoxically, the nature of the ministry can make it easy to avoid taking this responsibility. At seminary we are surrounded by professors and peers who stimulate us and encourage our spiritual growth. When we enter the local church, we discover that the people we serve often minister to us as much as we minister to them. Then there are colleagues and mentors, speakers and seminars, that contribute to our spiritual development. If we have a healthy marriage, our spouse will be a significant partner in the Christian journey.

Somewhere along the line, however, we have to own responsibility for the state of our soul—or we run the risk of one day looking into it and finding it empty. Accepting this ownership can be a wonderful but frightening step.

I've experienced several moments in my ministry

that raised questions within about my spiritual health. A few years ago I met with a group of high school seniors from our church. During a question-and-answer time, one guy asked, "Do you really believe all the stuff you say when you preach on Sunday morning? Do you have to have experienced the truths from the Bible that you're speaking on?"

I do not remember how I answered his question, but that was one event that triggered my reevaluation of the state of my soul. Pastors cannot experience every truth they preach, of course, but how often was I able to say, "I know this to be true because I've lived it"? I thought about the questions of that student for a long time.

I can still remember an Easter sermon I preached when I was thirty years old. The sermon included two great stories, one of which I knew would bring a tear to every eye. That Sunday the congregation was full, and I felt the air of excitement that comes upon a church in the spring—but as I preached I sensed within me very little spiritual passion. The week had been an emotional one for me. I had received a form letter from a search committee considering my résumé: *"You have wonderful gifts, but God has led us to a different person."*

I preached my Easter sermon knowing everything I said was true but there was no fire in my soul—even when using an emotional story to generate response. I felt as if I were delivering a lecture. I remember thinking, *Is this what happens when you get older? And what about when I hit fifty-five? Will I have to deal with this every week?*

In one of the lowest moments of my life, a church

member told me I was petty and did not evidence spiritual maturity. I felt sorry for myself, and my conversation with him revealed fear, cynicism, and unresolved anger. On the way home from that meeting, I rationalized all the reasons I had a right to be lagging in spiritual development. But soon I became convicted for blaming others for my lack and confessed my immature spirituality to the Lord. I also knew I had to confess this to the person who had made me aware of it.

I balked. How could I, the pastor, admit to my critic that I had been wrong? I did not even like this person. But I suppressed my ego, asked to see him, and said simply, "Your comments about my spiritual maturity were hard to take. But you were right."

Later when I told an older minister the story, he said, "The primary difference between the spiritually alive minister and one who died in his soul long before he was buried is the ability to say 'I'm sorry.'" It's doubly hard to say it at mid-life.

Spiritual authenticity and development do not come automatically with age. We know this, and may have preached on the subject, but it does not mean we will not wind up at mid-life bereft of vitality and spiritual passion. The good news is the best *can* be yet to come.

Holy man lessons

In 1983 I met a minister who exemplified spiritual authenticity. He pastored a rural congregation and asked me to conduct his church revival meetings—a very Baptist and very southern practice. He had a slight speech impediment and had suffered at the hands of his church constituents in ways most of us cannot imagine. I knew that some people in that church had deliberately tried to humiliate him and had not only crossed the line of public decency but had sinned against the man. In any other profession he would have had grounds for legal action, yet he stayed on as their pastor.

In all the revivals I have preached, I have never seen as much response as I did in that country church. I do not believe it was the result of my preaching or methods. Rather, the pastor had laid the foundation. I just happened to be the guy who could articulate some of what had been happening in the life of that church. There was the sense that God was honoring this truly holy man.

What made him what he was?

For one thing, he was publicly open about his feelings and insecurities. Rather than try to bluff his way through a situation, as so many tend to do, he admitted when he did not feel secure in a given area. He knew that because of his speech defect, the large pulpits would never be open to him. He was not as ambitious as I was, but he would be quick to admit that this lack of ambition was not necessarily a virtue, that he had to fight being satisfied with mediocrity. He wore his speech impediment as neither a crown nor a cross, but simply as a part of who he was.

His strong spiritual disciplines included prayer every day on his knees and Scripture read aloud from both

Testaments. He was the only pastor I had met up to that time who had a real "prayer closet"—a quiet place for himself and God alone. He never publicly trumpeted his prayer life, which I happened to know included reading prayers from the saints and writing his own prayers. This was unusual, given our Baptist tradition, which honors spontaneous spoken prayer.

That pastor modeled for me the connection between what I preach and what I experience. I had always worked hard on what I said and how I packaged it, but this man's desire was to live the truths of the gospel. He became a mentor to me, a long-distance coach.

Today we do not converse often but we do keep up with each other. He is now serving a church in a community that suffered severe economic devastation shortly after he arrived. He chose to walk with his people through the fire, turning down opportunities to leave. He felt his obligation was to stay and shepherd. Now the church and the community are feeling the frustration of numerical decline, and my friend is again facing tough days. But I know he will survive because he is a model of someone who has taken responsibility for his spirituality.

Looking for rainbows

My recurring theme here has been the temptation to give in to the entropy of age. Why create pain for ourselves at mid-life? Who wants to own up to the fact that while morally pure, we can be spiritual hypocrites?

When I was in my forties, I drifted into a spiritual twilight. I felt my prayers ineffectual and was spiritually numb. For several years I could see enough to move forward but not enough to function effectively. From the outside, I appeared to be the successful pastor of a large church. I had never violated my marriage vows, my wife and I had never been the subject of a scandal, and our three daughters gave evidence of vital relationships with God. From a financial perspective, we felt comfortable. But when I looked deep into my soul, I saw less than I wanted to see. I felt as if my soul had shriveled. What people saw outwardly did not match how I felt inwardly.

In May 1993 I had been at the church for less than two years. The move from Texas to Alabama had been more difficult for my family than I had anticipated. Mowing the lawn one morning, I began second-guessing our move: *Had I interpreted the will of God correctly?* I struggled under the assumption that if I were truly in God's will bad things would not happen to me. I began to feel sorry for myself and my family.

Yet the more I thought about it the more I felt convicted that my life was the opposite of what I preached. I had recently told my congregation in a sermon that you cannot measure the will of God by the circumstances of your life. The sermon drew a strong response—there were more requests for cassette copies than usual. That morning, rolling my lawn mower back into the garage, I made up my mind to never again feel sorry for myself about the move to Alabama—and that,

I discovered, was my first step out of my spiritual twilight.

The next incident happened almost four years later, in January 1997, when I was driving to another church to lead a retreat for church leaders. I felt discouraged because I was not as prepared as I wanted to be. Ministry emergencies and poor time management had destroyed my study time. And I felt I needed to review my material one more time.

In the car I listened to Harry Chapin, while kicking myself for not being better prepared. I was scheduled to lead a two-and-a-half-hour session that evening and another one the next morning. I sent up a prayer that God would help me deliver a good presentation in spite of myself: "Lord, I've got to have some help. Don't let me embarrass myself; more important, help me make a good presentation for the sake of those who have sacrificed their time to come to this retreat."

After my prayer I spotted in the distance a bright rainbow against the clouds. It had not been raining. It was as if God were saying, "Gary, it's going to be all right. The flood is past. Noah found grace and so will you." I have not had many such experiences before or since, but the moment affirmed me as a son of the Father. I came away with a deep sense of God's reassurance and presence: I could trust him even when I did not sense him near. God's grace extended even to preachers who mismanaged their time.

On a larger scale, I came away from that trip with the assurance that my years in the gloaming, in the spiritual twilight that had settled over my soul, were over. I finally understood that every day does not have to be sunny, that even when my soul feels shrouded in darkness, I know that God is still leading me. I do not need a clear day to feel confident God is leading me.

Big picture

The gifts of spiritual authenticity in mid-life—amid the loss and quiet desperation—are wisdom and perspective. We discover that even though circumstances change, God does not. He can be trusted. We become less result-oriented because we can look back and see that while some situations have not worked out, God is still at work. The work of the ministry is not solely on our shoulders. In our youth we see what we are doing for God, but as we grow older we see what God is doing through us.

For me, another gift of spiritual passion and health in mid-life has been less cynicism about local church work and a deeper conviction that I need the church more than it needs me. In a sense I have become "converted" to the church. I used to see it as a place to preach, an avenue for my ministry. Now I have begun to see it as more important than my individual ministry. The gospel tells us not only how to become a Christian but how to become part of the community of faith. Increasingly I find I need the fellowship of the saints, the singing of the hymns, the observance of the ordinances, the reading of the Scriptures—for my soul.

155

Richard Foster, author of *Celebration of Discipline* and *Prayer*, spoke at a conference at our church not long ago. While not as well attended as I had hoped it would be, the meetings attracted people from many denominations. I was impressed with how Foster endorsed all the authentic Christian traditions, identifying each as a stream in the great river of faith.

As I sat through the conference, my emotions moved from disappointment with the people who did not attend to surprise at those who did. By their presence they had brought to me a gift. I began to reflect upon how many streams of worship there are and the various churches I had served; each had contributed to my understanding of God, which can never be taken away. I was moved with gratitude for the variety that is in the body of Christ.

Now well into mid-life, I can say with conviction that God is clearly present. He is at work. It is well with my soul.

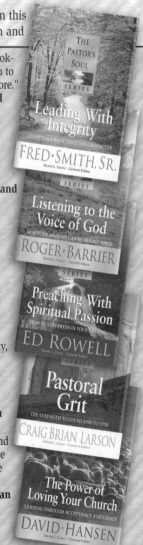

Thank you for selecting a book from
BETHANY HOUSE PUBLISHERS

Bethany House Publishers is a ministry of Bethany Fellowship
International, an interdenominational, nonprofit organization
committed to spreading the Good News of Jesus Christ around
the world through evangelism, church planting, literature
distribution, and care for those in need. Missionary training is
offered through Bethany College of Missions.

Bethany Fellowship International is a member of the National
Association of Evangelicals and subscribes to its statement of
faith. If you would like further information, please contact:

Bethany Fellowship International
6820 Auto Club Road
Minneapolis, MN 55438 USA